MACROBIOTIC PALM HEALING

Macrobiotic Palm Healing

Energy at Your Finger-Tips

Michio Kushi
with Olivia Oredson

Japan Publications, Inc.

Note to the reader: It is advisable to seek the guidance of a qualified health professional and macrobiotic counselor before implementing the dietary and other suggestions for specific conditions presented in this book. It is essential that any reader who has any reason to suspect serious illness in themselves or their family members seek appropriate advice promptly. Neither this or any other book should be used as a substitute for qualified care or treatment.

Published by
JAPAN PUBLICATIONS, INC., Tokyo and New York

Distributors:
UNITED STATES: *Kodansha International/USA, Ltd., through Harper & Row, Publishers, Inc., 599 Lexington Avenue, Suite 2300, New York, N. Y. 10022.* SOUTH AMERICA: *Harper & Row, Publishers, Inc., International Department.* CANADA: *Fitzhenry & Whiteside Ltd., 195 Allstate Parkway, Markham, Ontario, L3R 4T8.* MEXICO AND CENTRAL AMERICA: *HARLA S. A. de C. V., Apartado 30–546, Mexico 4, D. F.* BRITISH ISLES: *Premier Book Marketing Ltd., 1 Gower Street, London WC1E 6HA.* EUROPEAN CONTINENT: *European Book Service PBD, Strijkviertel 63, 3454 PK De Meern, The Netherlands.* AUSTRALIA AND NEW ZEALAND: *Bookwise International, 54 Crittenden Road, Findon, South Australia 5007.* THE FAR EAST AND JAPAN: *Japan Publications Trading Co., Ltd., 1–2–1, Sarugaku-cho, Chiyoda-ku, Tokyo 101.*

First edition: December 1988

LCCC 86–081326
ISBN 0–87040–672–8

Printed U.S.A.

Dedication

To those persons,
Past, present and future,
For whom healing
Is the primary focus of life,
And whose spirit
Has inspired this writing.

Olivia Oredson
Holderness, New Hampshire

Foreword

Modern conventional medicine and other health approaches have their limitations as everyone recognizes. The limitations are based upon the lack of understanding of humanity. Humanity is related not only to physical matter but also to all cosmological factors including vibration, energy, and waves. All physical phenomena, and related movement and behavior and all psychological phenomena, and related images and thoughts, are largely composed of moving currents of vibrational energy which come from the external environment to the center of the body and burst out from the body toward the external environment. The Japanese word for sickness is *byo-ki* (disturbed energy); all human affairs can be oriented, directed, and governed by vibrational movement. Without understanding, it is difficult to administer human health and achieve the development of humanity.

Olivia Oredson, who compiled, edited, refined, and composed this *Book of Palm Healing* has developed a profound understanding of the nature of humanity in terms of vibration and energy. She has studied with me for more than fifteen years; she has taught cooking and palm healing on various occasions to many people. She also contributed as my assistant in writing *The Book of Macrobiotics*, the original version, and *The Book of Dō-In*, both published by Japan Publications, Inc. She also was the educational director of The Kushi Institute in Brookline, Massachusetts, when it was established in 1980. Although many of the contents Olivia has dealt with in this book were taught by me in the past to the public, she has also developed her own understanding and technique through her well-mastered comprehension of human energy structure and energetic movement.

Palm Healing is a unique art of healing. It is unique because it is very natural, intuitive, instructive, and harmless. It has been practiced in daily life since the beginning of the human race through natural daily behavior. When it is known why "palm healing" or "laying of the hands" can relieve various physical disorders and can serve in the development of humanity toward heightening spiritual nature, the practice of palm healing will become very useful for day to day life among people.

I sincerely hope everyone, regardless of their occupation, age, race, and belief, will benefit from the *Book of Palm Healing*; it has been presented in a clean, simple, and well-written presentation by Olivia Oredson.

I further extend my sincere appreciation to Edward Esko, a teacher at The Kushi Institute for his help in reviewing the manuscript and to Japan Publications, Inc., for publishing this book.

Michio Kushi
August 1988
Brookline, Massachusetts

Preface and Acknowledgments

Palm healing is a wonderful healing art that is easy and enjoyable to use. This book was written in order to share the clear, comprehensive method of palm healing taught by Michio Kushi, foremost teacher of the macrobiotic diet and way of life. Mr. Kushi and his wife Aveline have published many books on diet, cooking, Oriental diagnosis, child care, and other subjects related to this healthful, wholistic lifestyle. Palm healing is also an integral part of the macrobiotic approach, and this is the first time that Mr. Kushi's teachings on palm healing have been published in detail.

While practicing the macrobiotic diet and way of life for the past nineteen years, first as a student of the Kushis and then as a teacher, I have gained an appreciation for the art of palm healing and its value as part of a natural, healthful way of life. After attending Mr. Kushi's classes, I began to practice palm healing frequently, and found it to be extremely useful for personal health care, for myself and for those with whom I practiced it. Palm healing is a gentle, subtle art, but surprisingly effective and with a long-lasting effect. It benefits the body, and also the mind and emotions. There have been many times when the use of simple palm-healing practices has been able to reduce pain, increase strength and energy, alleviate stress, and give comfort.

Perhaps best of all, palm healing is such a natural and simple art that it can be done by almost anyone, and for almost anyone. The study of palm healing helps to reconnect us with our natural healing abilities, our birthright as human beings.

The idea for this book came as a result of the interest of students in palm healing classes that I taught in recent years at the Kushi Institute in Boston. These students were very interested in reading books to learn more about palm healing, and I felt sorry that there was no book that described Mr. Kushi's teachings about palm healing, on which I was basing the classes. I thought that I should write a short study guide outlining the practices. When I talked with Edward Esko and Alex Jack, macrobiotic teachers and authors, they suggested that it should be a complete book rather than a short guide. It is due to the interest of the students and the suggestions of Mr. Esko and Mr. Jack that this book came into being, and I want to thank them for their part. Mr. Esko and Mr. Jack also gave me a great deal of advice and guidance regarding the book production, and Mr. Esko reviewed the manuscript more than once.

Material for the book was drawn from numerous lectures, seminars, and classes given by Michio Kushi on the subject of palm healing for nearly the past two decades, in his teaching centers in Boston, Brookline, and Becket, Massachusetts, as well as abroad. Part of this information was taken from the course plans Mr. Kushi designed in 1978 and 1979 for the Kushi Institute classes in palm healing, and training information given to me and Rodney House, macrobiotic teacher, at that time to prepare us for teaching the course.

After receiving an introduction to palm healing in Mr. Kushi's seminars, my own interest in the subject grew, and I studied several other methods of palm healing over the years. Space does not permit naming them, but I am grateful to these additional teachers for their guidance which has contributed to my understanding of palm healing.

The palm healing workshops given by Mrs. Lima Ohsawa on her brief visits to Boston have been an inspiration as well. Mrs. Ohsawa also wrote articles about palm healing which appeared in books that are currently out of print, and her late husband, George Ohsawa, spoke about palm healing in his own teachings. Mr. and Mrs. Ohsawa are the founders of the macrobiotic movement, and Mrs. Ohsawa continues to teach and inspire even today at her advanced age. I am grateful to both of them for their influence.

I would like to acknowledge Ms. Shizuko Yamamoto as a guiding light in the field of shiatsu massage and macrobiotic palm healing, and thank her for her teaching on these subjects for many years. Her influence can certainly be felt throughout this book.

Ms. Cecile Levin, macrobiotic teacher, and Ms. Betsy Polatin, teacher of the Alexander Technique and macrobiotic practitioner, have shared with me their knowledge of macrobiotic palm healing along with their advice, guidance, and friendship, and I wish to thank them for their help. I would also like to thank my good friends Margaret Braxton, Beth Fisher, Linda Hamelin, and Janet Jagodzinski for their advice, encouragement, and discussions about healing which were invaluable during the creation of this book.

In order to give a clear picture of Michio Kushi's teachings on palm healing, I have organized them in much the same way he used to do in his two-day palm healing seminars of the early 1970s. In some places I have added my own interpretations and innovations when it seemed that they would make comprehension better for the reader, but I have tried to avoid introducing any changes that would hinder rather than help the presentation of Mr. Kushi's central ideas.

Something that is difficult to duplicate in writing, however, is the *spirit* and *energy* of those original seminars, which were always so entertaining and enlivening. Mr. Kushi is known to be an inspired—and inspiring—teacher, and these palm healing seminars were no exception. They would often take on an almost musical quality, and Mr. Kushi would lead the students from one exercise to the next almost like the conductor of an orchestra swinging into one number after another. Bit by bit our spirits and energy would rise so that by the end of the seminar, even the most tired and discouraged person was able to spring down the street with a big smile! I hope that this book has been able to do justice to the original, at least in some respects.

The production of a single book involves a surprisingly large number of people. In addition to those already named, I would like to acknowledge the people whose time and energy have gone into this book's creation, and there are even more who cannot be named to lack of space.

I would like to thank Mr. Yoshiro Fujiwara and Mr. Iwao Yoshizaki of Japan Publications, Inc., for agreeing to publish the book and for their patience, guidance, and advice during the long process of book production.

The artist who created the expert drawings is Mr. Christian Gauthier of Boston and I would like to thank him for his participation. Mr. Kushi provided the illustrations of points in Chapter 7. I wish to thank Mr. Christopher Triplett, photographer of Marblehead, Massachusetts, for his fine work and for his advice and guidance regarding the photos. The models who gave their time and energy are Steve Cohen and Pauline Kenny, Kushi Institute students during 1987, who appear in the majority of the chapters; Ms. Lillian Barsevick (with short hair), long-time macrobiotic teacher, and Ms. Diane Scanzani (with dark hair), Kushi Foundation staff member, who appear in Chapters 3, 5 and 11; and students and friends of the Kushi Institute, autumn 1987, who appear in the group pictures in Chapter 11. I would like to thank all of these people for their cheerful and patient participation. The Kushi Institute and the Sei Shoku Aikikai of Brookline, Massachusetts, provided studio space and staff support for the photo sessions.

My husband Jack Saunders exhibited great patience during the long months of book writing and I wish to express my gratitude to him for this, as well as for his advice and help in certain phases of book production. My parents, Mr. and Mrs. Oliver and Irma Oredson of Minneapolis, Minnesota, have been generous with their advice and encouragement as they always have done, and I would like to express my thanks to them for their help.

Michio Kushi, through his tireless teaching for many years, has brought us this wonderful healing information. He has set an example for us all through his hard work and dedication, and I would like to thank him for his inspiration and guidance which made this book possible.

May you, the reader, find this information on palm healing helpful, and may you use it throughout life in good health and happiness.

Olivia Oredson
Holderness, New Hampshire.

Contents

14

Chapter 1
What Is Palm Healing?

Our hands have the power to heal. For as long as there has been recorded history, humankind has known and used this natural ability. Remarkable and mysterious as the stars, yet as familiar and commonplace as a stone—the energy that flows through our hands has the power to help and to give care.

Who has not noticed the power of touch? A friend places a hand on our shoulder, and a feeling of reassurance flows through us. A child cries, and we place a hand on her back to give a feeling of calm and stability. A strong handshake seems to say "Have courage!" and we remember it for hours afterward. A sudden headache—our first act is to place our hand on the painful area. We do these things without thinking, for they are natural actions, the almost instinctive use of our healing ability.

Everyone can learn to use the hands for healing, even young children. It does not require complicated training, expensive equipment or unusual qualifications. By following some simple rules and principles, you can uncover this ability in yourself and use it to help family and friends.

Hands Around the World

For many centuries, the art of palm healing has been practiced in many parts of the world, as shown in ancient literature, artwork and traditions that have been handed down to the present day. Let us look at some of these traditional uses of palm healing.

The Orient. In Japan, *te-ate,* "hand application," and *tanasue-no-michi,* "the *Tao* of placing hands," have been known for centuries. Thousands of years before the Christian era, shiatsu massage and acupuncture developed in China and Japan, based upon a fundamental awareness of our energy flow which had been gained by practicing by hand. All of these applications utilized the same understanding of our body's energy system of meridians and points, as we will describe in Chapter 2. That this understanding also existed in India is evidenced by the discovery of ancient maps of the human body showing the meridians and points —pathways and concentrations of energy used by practitioners of natural medicine. Palm healing, massage, and yoga were natural healing arts practiced by the ancient Indians and Tibetans.

Throughout Asia, palm healing practices have been associated both with the healing arts of medicine, and with religious traditions of prayer and blessing. Notice the hand positions, for example, of the statues of Buddhist saints pictured in books of Oriental art. The hands of such figures are often held in poses that suggest sending or radiating a healing force.

16

Egypt and Greece. The Egyptians used palm healing as a medical treatment in very early times, before 1550 B.C., as we know from writings in early literature. In Greece, palm healing was also used in very early times and was documented by Aristophanes in the fourth century B.C.[1] The natural medicine practiced by these ancient civilizations utilized an understanding of energy flowing through the whole of nature, of which human beings are a part. Often the medical and religious practices were closely interwoven, and there was little or no distinction drawn between physical and spiritual well-being.

Palm healing has been practiced through the ages in many parts of the world.

[1] Bernard Grad, "Healing by the Laying on of Hands: A Review of Experiments" in *Ways of Health* edited by David S. Sobel (New York and London: Harcourt Brace Jovanovich, 1979).

Judaism and Christianity.   For several centuries before Christ, palm healing was practiced by the Hebrew people. It was used in Judaism as a ritual for consecration and transmitting divine healing power.[2] Jesus carried on this tradition, using palm healing frequently for healing in both the physical and spiritual sense. There are many remarkable passages in the New Testament illustrating Jesus's use of palm healing. For example, Luke 4: 40 says:

> Now when the sun was setting, all they that had any sick with divers diseases brought them unto him; and he laid his hands on every one of them, and healed them.

Additional passages abound in the New Testament illustrating Jesus's use of palm healing. Following are some interesting examples to look up: Matthew 8: 14–15; 14: 14; Mark 1: 40–42; 5: 25–29; 6: 5; 7: 32–35; 8: 22–25; and Luke 5: 12–13.

Africa.   African civilizations have utilized the art of palm healing for many generations, as we know from the verbally transmitted histories that have been passed down through the years. As in many other traditional cultures, palm healing in Africa has represented a combination of the medical and religious, physical and spiritual practices. The general population used palm healing, but particularly respected the healing done by specially trained medice men and women. This natural medicine followed the Africans who moved to the Western Hemisphere, and such palm healing practices may be found today in certain parts of the Caribbean and the southern United States. In parts of Africa as yet unaffected by modern civilization, these original traditions are still alive.

Europe.   The church was king in early and medieval Europe, and palm healing was practiced by clergy in both churches and synagogues as a religious ritual. In addition, in many countries, royalty were regarded as divine representatives, and it was thought that a touch from their hand would promote healing. Medieval literature and drawings show European kings giving their subjects the "king's touch," laying their hands on the head or shoulders of those who came for healing.[3]

In eighteenth and nineteenth century Europe, palm healing became the subject of scientific interest. A researcher named Franz Mesmer developed a theory that a "magnetic fluid" exists in our body which is responsible for conditions of health and disease, and which responds to palm healing. His theory was accepted by the French Academie des Sciences in 1831.[4] Mesmer did many experiments and developed a practice based upon this "magnetism," as he called it. A number of other researchers were doing similar work around the same time. Unfortunately, popular

---

[2] Encyclopedia Britannica, 1977

[3] "English kings and queens were reputed to have the power of healing. Special audiences were given for the sick to receive the 'king's touch.' " Frances Kennett, *Folk Medicine* N.Y.: Crescent Books, 1976).

[4] Bernard Grad, *Ibid.*

interest reduced these ideas to the level of parlor games in many instances and created a reputation of occultism in the process.

America.   European explorers who traveled in America in the sixteenth and early seventeenth centuries reported that Native Americans, both North and South, practiced healing by touch or palm healing. American Indian culture is based in a deep understanding and respect for nature and the interaction of humanity with nature. The natural energies which flow through all plants, animals, and humans are seen as manifestations of the Great Spirit, and all are unified as one. Special techniques of massage and palm healing were known to certain tribes, and are still practiced today among those who preserve their traditional heritage, which is handed down orally from elders to youths.

   Among the European settlers who came to America, the Shakers, a Christian religious community, practiced laying-on-of-hands as a religious observance and for healing. Their name derives from their tendency to move and shake as a result of the electromagnetic current that flowed through them during the healing process.

Modern Developments.   Since 1900, scientists have shown increasing interest in investigating the nature of the energy used in palm healing and other related practices. In the 1930s, Wilhelm Reich worked with healing energy which he called *orgone*. He created an "orgone box" designed to concentrate life energy for the benefit of the person sitting inside. Reich did a great deal of work researching and writing about the nature and uses of this energy. In Russia, *Kirlian photography* was invented, utilizing special equipment able to photograph the energy itself emanating from people, animals, plants, and even inanimate objects. Researchers have been able to use Kirlian photography to document changes in life energy resulting from the addition of a controlled stimulus.

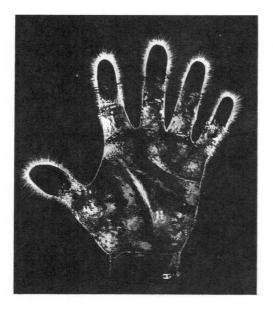

Kirlian photography is able to show the energy around a person or object, much as we see in this illustration.

In Japan, several new methods of palm healing have emerged in modern times. *Reiki*, a popular method, meaning "Spiritual Energy," was developed by Dr. Mikao Usui in the late 1800s and early 1900s. Two more methods, *Johrei* ("Purification of Spirit") and *Mahikari* ("True Light"), have developed more recently. All of these are widely used not only in Japan but around the world. Additional methods may also be found.

In America, researchers Dora Kunz and Dolores Krieger, R. N., Ph.D. developed a practice called Therapeutic Touch after observing the palm healing practices of a gentleman who had developed the ability to heal with his hands, and who spent many years helping both people and animals. Therapeutic Touch is widely taught and practiced by both nurses and lay persons.[5]

With the advent of modern wholistic and New Age philosophies, popular interest has grown in the art of palm healing. Ancient traditions have been unearthed, traditional folk practices have been revived, all updated for modern purposes. Increasing scientific interest is leading to controlled experiments and the collection of data which can help to guide and form our future practice as well.[6] We will be able to add the time-tested art of palm healing to our repertoire of health practices, and the benefit of centuries of human experience can be right at our fingertips.

The Macrobiotic Approach to Palm Healing

The founder of modern macrobiotics, George Ohsawa, used the traditional Japanese practice of *te-ate* (hand-healing) as one aspect of the healthful way of life that he taught. Mr. Ohsawa and his wife Lima Ohsawa taught palm healing in Japan and then spread their teachings to Europe and the United States. I have continued to practice and teach palm healing in Boston and on a world-wide scale. As a result of these teachings, as well as the efforts of macrobiotic associates throughout the world, numerous students of the macrobiotic way of life now practice the art of palm healing as an everyday activity.

The understanding that we are energy, and that by working with our own energy flow we can improve our well-being, is a commonly accepted idea in macrobiotic philosophy. Using palm healing is common sense, and macrobiotic philosophy offers guidelines for its practice.

The many palm healing techniques that are taught today around the world provide inspiration and a wonderful selection of methods to draw from. It is possible to become confused, however, by the contradictions and differences that exist among these many techniques. For example, one school of thought says that it is important to hold your hands still at one location while giving palm healing, while

---

5 Dolores Krieger, R. N., Ph. D., *The Therapeutic Touch: How to Use Your Hands to Help or to Heal* (New Jersey: Prentice-Hall, Inc., 1976).

6 Dolores Krieger, "High-Order Emergence of the Self During Therapeutic Touch," *The American Theosophist* magazine (May 1984).
  Dora Kunz and Erik Peper, "Fields and Their Clinical Implications," *The American Theosophist* magazine (1982, two-part article).

another method claims that to hold your hands still is an error, and that we should keep our hands moving at all times. These two methods are in obvious contradiction, yet both are very popular and have thousands of adherents. How can both methods be correct? How can we choose between them?

The macrobiotic approach offers an answer. The unifying principle of *yin* and *yang*, known since ancient times in the Orient, is used in the macrobiotic way of life to understand things which are seemingly contradictory or opposing. Yin represents expansive, centrifugal force, and all tendencies and movements associated with it; yang represents contractive, centripetal force and all tendencies and movements associated with it. (These will be explained in more detail shortly.) By understanding the yin and yang nature of each method of palm healing, we can see the value in each one, and determine which method is most appropriate to use in which set of circumstances. It is thus not necessary to utilize only one method or technique and reject the others: with understanding, we can appreciate all techniques, utilizing and harmonizing them as needed in our practice.

In order to accomplish this, we need a good working understanding of yin and yang, and we need a good sense of discernment—which is the result of an alert, healthy condition of body and mind.

The Function of Palm Healing

What is the role of palm healing in relation to other methods of health care? Palm healing works with the cause of our physical and mental condition —our underlying energy flow. Since it does not use any special equipment, it is inexpensive and economical, and can be done almost anywhere by anyone. It is gentle, safe, and does not produce undesirable side-effects, yet in its subtle way it is powerful and effective. Palm healing may be used in a light, brief manner for quick care, or in a more lengthy and intensive session for stronger care.

The chart in Fig. 1:1 illustrates the relative effectiveness of various methods of health care, from the natural macrobiotic point of view, evaluated according to their comprehensiveness and their degree of side effects. At the top, our View of Life reflects our total orientation to ourselves and the world, and is thus an all-pervasive influence on our life and health. From our View of Life we determine our diet (the next line), which has an underlying, controlling effect upon our entire health condition, mind and body. After diet, the next most influential and effective daily health practices are Dō-In and palm healing—self-care through massage and energy work. Constantly adjusting, constantly aware of our energy condition throughout the day, we are able to exert a subtly controlling influence on our well-being.

Using the proper practice of diet, palm healing, and Dō-In on a regular basis, we have a complete system of health maintenance and may not need to bring in other methods. Historically, these were the earliest methods developed for health care. Practiced from birth (and before birth via the mother and father), they acted as lifelong preventive and maintenance health measures.

When balance has been disturbed, however, we may need additional types of treatment and the next category is brought into play. Examples range from meditation through martial arts, the introspective through the active, with some being more yin and some being more yang. These techniques developed historically later than palm healing, Dō-In, and diet. They are natural, generally safe techniques although less directly affecting the cause of our condition and not as comprehensive for basic care. These methods began to come into use after the understanding of diet began to decline in very ancient times.

The next category, including herbal medicine, can be brought into play when the condition has become more out-of-balance and requires a stronger, quicker form of treatment. These methods are based on natural principles, but can produce greater side effects than those listed above.

The final category, including surgery and chemical medicines, is for emergencies when there is a severe imbalance, and a very quick, strong treatment is needed. This category is the most disruptive to our body and mind and produces the greatest side effects; it is also the least economical. We may need to use such emergency measures in the event of a severe health crisis, although we may often regret the disturbing side effects eventually.

Perspective on Palm Healing

Palm healing is most effective when used on a regular basis over a period of time, producing an ongoing and consistent effect on our energy flow. Certainly we can obtain a good effect from a single application of palm healing, but we cannot expect

Fig. 1:1
The Relative Effectiveness of Health Care Methods

VIEW OF LIFE

DIET

DO-IN   PALM HEALING

Meditation—Meditation and—Acupuncture—Moxi-   —Shiatsu—Yoga—Martial Arts
Chanting   bustion

YIN   YANG

Herbal Medicine   Compresses and   Folk Treatments
Poultices

Surgery   Chemical Medicine,   Symptomatic
Pills, Injections   Treatments

From our View of Life is derived our diet (diet also influences the View of Life). Then the practices differentiate into yin and yang: Do-In done individually, palm healing usually with a partner. From these developed either their combination or variation: massage, etc. Then the short-term symptomatic herbal and folk medicines. At the bottom are practices used frequently today but which we would reccommend to use only as needed for emergency situations, since they often include harmful side effects.

just one session to solve all problems. Human conditions of health and sickness result from many days, months, or years of development, and cannot be changed in one hour. Nor can we expect palm healing to work miraculous cures. The accounts in the New Testament of Jesus performing instantaneous cures through palm healing are to be admired, but in most circumstances we cannot expect to immediately duplicate these results. A serious health condition may be aided by palm healing, but it is important to give other care as needed, and in an emergency situation when medical care is required, to attend to the medical necessities first.

By making palm healing a regular part of our daily life, over time we generate cumulative results. With experience, the practice of palm healing can become more powerful and focused, increasing in effectiveness as the years pass. In the context of a healthful way of life and good diet, the effectiveness of palm healing can be multiplied manyfold, and even in the beginning important benefits can result.

The Compass of Yin and Yang

Decisions about palm healing such as determining the condition of the receiving person, knowing what result is to be desired, and deciding what technique is appropriate for the situation, can be approached by an understanding of yin and yang. This ancient philosophy provides a clear and easy method of seeing through problems and deciding what to do whether we are talking about diet, palm healing, flower arranging, or anything else. The terms yin and yang come from the Orient, but a similar understanding is found in some form in most traditional cultures.[7] It is the idea of making harmony between opposites—night and day, light and dark, fast and slow, hot and cold. Yin and yang refer to these opposite qualities:

Yin	Yang
Expansion	Contraction
Cold	Hot
Dark	Bright
Slow	Fast
Night	Day
Female	Male
Upward motion	Downward motion
Soft	Hard
Passive	Aggressive
Negative charge	Positive charge

A more detailed list is shown in Fig. 1:2. All objects or activities can be described in terms of yin and yang, and have a combination of yin and yang qualities. For example, a person may be active (yang) and yet somewhat depressed (yin). We are made up of a combination of these energies. For that reason, no person or object

[7] One example is the qualities *rajas-tamas-sattva* used in Indian philosophy.

Fig. 1:2 *Detailed Examples of Yin and Yang*

	YIN ▽*	YANG △*
Attribute	Centrifugal force	Centripetal force
Tendency	Expansion	Contraction
Function	Diffusion	Fusion
	Dispersion	Assimilation
	Separation	Gathering
	Decomposition	Organization
Movement	More inactive, slower	More active, faster
Vibration	Shorter wave and higher frequency	Longer wave and lower frequency
Direction	Ascent and vertical	Descent and horizontal
Position	More outward and peripheral	More inward and central
Weight	Lighter	Heavier
Temperature	Colder	Hotter
Light	Darker	Brighter
Humidity	Wetter	Drier
Density	Thinner	Thicker
Size	Larger	Smaller
Shape	More expansive and fragile	More contractive and harder
Form	Longer	Shorter
Texture	Softer	Harder
Atomic particle	Electron	Proton
Elements	N, O, P, Ca, etc.	H, C, Na, As, Mg, etc.
Environment	Vibration ... Air ... Water ... Earth	
Climatic effects	Tropical climate	Colder climate
Biological	More vegetable quality	More animal quality
Sex	Female	Male
Organ structure	More hollow and expansive	More compacted and condensed
Nerves	More peripheral, orthosympathetic	More central, parasympathetic
Attitude, emotion	More gentle, negative, defensive	More active, postive, aggressive
Work	More psychological and mental	More physical and social
Consciousness	More universal	More specific
Mental function	Dealing more with the future	Dealing more with the past
Culture	More spiritually oriented	More materially oriented
Dimension	Space	Time

* For convenience, the symbols ▽ for Yin, and △ for Yang are used.

can be completely yang or completely yin, but can be more yang or more yin than someone else. Person A may be more yang than person B, but more yin than person C.

In order to be healthy, we need to have both yin and yang traits, well-balanced and in good proportion.

The principles by which the qualities or energies of yin and yang operate are summarized in the list in Fig. 1:3. These principles offer to everyone the challenge

Fig. 1:3   *The Principles by Which Yin and Yang Operate*

Seven Principles of the Order of the Universe
1. All things are differentiated apparatus of One Infinity.
2. Everything changes.
3. All antagonisms are complementary.
4. There is nothing identical.
5. What has a front has a back.
6. The bigger the front, the bigger the back.
7. What has a beginning has an end.

Twelve Theorems of the Unifying Principle
1. One Infinity differentiates itself into yin and yang which are the poles that come into operation when the infinite centrifugality arrives at the geometric point of bifurcation.
2. Yin and yang result continuously from the infinite centrifugality.
3. Yin is centrifugal. Yang is centripetal. Yin and yang together produce energy and all phenomena.
4. Yin attracts yang. Yang attracts yin.
5. Yin repels yin. Yang repels yang.
6. The force of attraction and repulsion is proportional to the difference of the yin and yang components. Yin and yang combined in varying proportions produce energy and all phenomena.
7. All phenomena are ephemeral, constantly changing their constitution of yin and yang components.
8. Nothing is solely yin or solely yang. Everything involves polarity.
9. There is nothing neuter. Either yin or yang is in excess in every occurrence.
10. Large yin attracts small yin. Large yang attracts small yang.
11. At the extremes, yin produces yang, and yang produces yin.
12. All physical forms and objects are yang at the center and yin at the surface.

of a lifetime of fascinating study. The application of these principles is endless, leading from one engrossing discovery to the next.

A better understanding of yin and yang grows with practice, and may be assisted by attending classes and reading books on that subject. Suggestions are offered in the bibliography.

Yin and Yang in Palm Healing

The objective of palm healing is to bring about a state of greater harmony in our physical and mental condition. Yin and yang energies are harmonized, and as a result, tendencies to be too yin or too yang are tempered. Illness may be seen as imbalance, when either yin or yang qualities have become excessive. The list that follows gives examples of traits that people exhibit when they have excessively yin or yang energy.

A balanced person, on the other hand, would have an alert nature, flexibly responding to situations as needed.

Since our condition is in a state of constant change, it is impossible to achieve an absolute, perfect balance. However, we can become more balanced so that we

Too Yin	Too Yang
Passive	Aggressive
Overly relaxed	Tense
Inactive, lazy	Overactive
Depressed, sad	Angry, irritable
Negative, retreating	Attacking, intolerant
Self-pity	Self-pride
Voice too soft, timid	Voice too loud, tense
Loose muscles	Tight muscles
Moist skin	Dry skin

experience fewer swings in mood and physical condition, through regulation of our diet and lifestyle, and with the help of palm healing practice.

In order to help balance someone's condition through palm healing, we need to adjust the type of palm healing given to suit the receiver's condition. For example:

Present Condition	Desired Result	Type of Palm Healing Needed
Too yin, not enough yang energy	Become less yin and more yang	Yangizing methods
Too yang, not enough yin energy	Become less yang and more yin	Yinnizing methods
Both too yin and too yang qualities are present	Reduce and harmonize extremes	Both yang and yin harmonizing, centering methods
Not enough of either yin or yang qualities	Increase both types of energy	Both yin and yang harmonizing, energizing methods

A *yangizing* method would be one which produces more activity, heat, and tightness in the person; a *yinnizing* method would produce more relaxation, coolness, and quietness. Both types of care have their usefulness and are needed in different situations, and for different conditions. Yin and yang factors will be discussed throughout the book in relation to the various palm healing exercises, but some of the more important ones are:

	Yin Method	Yang Method
Hand movements:	Slower	Faster
Direction:	Up (toe to head) Out (Inside to outside)	Down (head to toe) In (Outside to inside)
Breathing pattern:	Slow, upward	Fast, downward

Many other variables influence the nature of palm healing and will be discussed in later chapters.

Yin and yang energy also change according to influences from the environment such as time of day, season, climate, and activity. These factors can also have a bearing on the type of palm healing that is called for:

Factor:		Palm healing should be:
Time of day:	Noon (yang)	More yin
	Midnight (yin)	More yang
	Sunrise (balanced/yang)	Balanced, toward yin
	Sunset (balanced/yin)	Balanced, toward yang
Climate:	Cold/winter (yin)	More yang
	Hot/summer (yang)	More yin
	Autumn (balanced/yin)	Balanced, toward yang
	Spring (balanced/yang)	Balanced, toward yin
Moon phase:	Full moon (yang)	More yin
	New moon (yin)	More yang
	Waxing moon (balanced/yang)	Balanced, toward yin
	Waning moon (balanced/yin)	Balanced, toward yang
Environment:	City (more yang)	More yin
	Country (more yin)	More yang
Activity:	Busy life (yang)	More yin
	Quiet life (yin)	More yang

Referring to the list of yin and yang qualities in Fig. 1:2, it is possible to add many more examples of factors influencing us and to make corresponding adjustments as needed in palm healing methods.

Intuitive vesus Analytical Approach to Palm Healing

We human beings are endowed with a remarkable intuitive faculty, and this is fully utilized in palm healing, as is our analytical ability. Let us put this relationship into perspective.

The principles of yin and yang are very useful tools. With yin and yang, it becomes easier to understand each person's condition and the type of palm healing needed. The basic guidelines presented in this chapter can serve as a starting point for developing better understanding of this philosophy and its application to healing. Naturally, this takes time. However, it is possible to begin understanding yin and yang by reflecting on these principles and noticing how they operate in daily life. We can also begin to apply these principles in the practice of palm healing.

The principles of yin and yang describe the operation of natural phenomena. They are not rules that are followed by people and things in the sense that we follow the rules of a city or a country. Rather, they are observations of the way things operate. In using yin and yang, it is important to continue this attitude of observation and experimentation, and to maintain flexibility. Nature is always moving, and always changing. Yin and yang—the laws of change—help us understand events, sometimes in retrospect. Yin and yang can be used for guidance.

In practicing palm healing, as in many other areas of life, it often happens that we experience a strong intuition that leaps over or bypasses intellectual analysis. This natural, instinctive or intuitive ability develops further as we become healthier and more alert through a good-quality diet and lifestyle, and it increases with practice and experience. As we become more aware, we begin to directly perceive energy flow, and can automatically give the appropriate type of palm healing, without thinking about it. To develop this ability may take years, although some people may develop it more quickly.

To do palm healing well, we need both abilities—our intuition or instinct, and our ability to think and analyze. All of our faculties should be working together harmoniously: We need to be healthy and well-balanced, physically and mentally. In order to be healthy, we need to pay attention to our basic way of life and diet—important factors that determine our health condition and energy flow. When giving palm healing care to others, we need to be in a clear, strong condition in order to think and perceive well, and in order to be a good transmitter of healing energy. When we are on the receiving end of palm healing, we will benefit all the more if we are healthy and clear enough to take in and process the energy that is given to us.

Diet and Way of Life

A healthy mind in a healthy body: for thousands of years, wise men and women have taught that this is achieved through regulation of our diet and daily life, as well as by the quality of our thoughts. It appears that in modern times, many people have forgotten this time-proven wisdom. However, it is never too late for us to regain this understanding and put it to use to raise our level of health and happiness. The macrobiotic approach to diet and lifestyle is a modern expression of these principles.

Public awareness is increasingly in accord with principles of diet and lifestyle that macrobiotics has taught for many decades. A great deal of attention is being given today to the importance of a good diet—reducing fat intake, reducing chemically-treated and refined foods, reducing the amount of rich foods and sugary desserts, and cutting down on alcohol, caffeine, and excessive salt. Increased use of foods high in fiber, fresh vegetables and fruits, whole grains and beans, low-fat fish, non-stimulant beverages, and other natural products, is commonly recommended. Everyone now knows the importance of exercise and fresh air, as well as positive thought patterns for stress reduction.

The macrobiotic approach offers an even more detailed and refined understanding, one that allows us to regulate these factors according to individual needs and for specific results. With an understanding of yin and yang, we can see the usefulness of each type of food, and balance different food qualities with the yin and yang factors in the environment. We can further work with the yin and yang qualities of foods through careful choice of cooking methods. Food, along with lifestyle, thus becomes one of the most important means of guiding our own health condition toward more yin or yang state, a more physical or spiritual orientation, a more active or receptive condition, according to the type of activity we wish to pursue and the type of qualities we wish to engender.

Because of the great importance of diet and way of life for our health, and as a basis for a good practice of palm healing, we recommend a more detailed study of these factors. Sources for further reading and classes are listed in the bibliography. Cooking classes given by qualified teachers are most helpful for learning how to create a proper diet. Following is a summary of the most important principles of the macrobiotic diet and way of life.

Macrobiotic Recommendations for Diet and Lifestyle

1. Whole cereal grains. At least 50 percent by volume of every meal is recommended to include cooked, organically grown, whole cereal grains prepared in a variety of ways. Whole cereal grains include brown rice, barley, millet, oats, corn, rye, wheat, and buckwheat. Please note that a small portion of this amount may consist of noodles or pasta, unyeasted whole-grain breads, and other partially processed whole cereal grains.

2. Soups. Approximately 5 to 10 percent of your daily food intake may include soup made with vegetables, sea vegetables (*wakame* or *kombu*), grains, or beans. Seasonings are usually *miso* or *tamari* soy sauce. The flavor should not be too salty.

3. Vegetables. About 20 to 30 percent of daily intake may include local and organically grown vegetables. Preferably, the majority are cooked in various styles (e.g., sautéed with a small amount of sesame or corn oil, steamed, boiled, and sometimes prepared using tamari soy sauce or light sea salt as a seasoning). A small

Fig. 1:4
Recommended Dietary Proportions

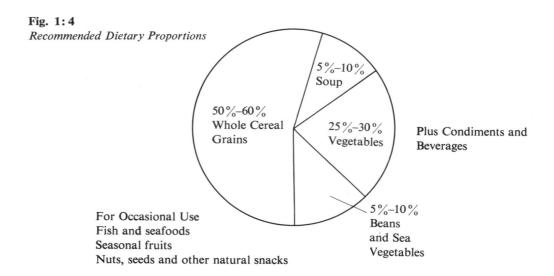

portion may be eaten as raw salad. Pickled vegetables without spice may also be used daily in small volume.

Vegetables for daily use include green cabbage, kale, broccoli, cauliflower, collards, pumpkin, watercress, Chinese cabbage, bok choy, dandelion, mustard greens, *daikon* greens, scallion, onions, daikon, turnips, acorn squash, butternut squash, buttercup squash, burdock, carrots, and other seasonally available varieties.

Avoid potatoes (including sweet potatoes and yams), tomatoes, eggplant, peppers, asparagus, spinach, beets, zucchini, and avocado from regular use. Mayonnaise and other oily dressings should be avoided.

4. Beans and sea vegetables. Approximately 5 to 10 percent of our daily diet includes cooked beans and sea vegetables. The most suitable beans for regular use are *azuki* beans, chick-peas, and lentils. Other beans may be used on occasion. Bean products such as *tofu, tempeh,* and *natto* can also be used. Sea vegetables such as *nori,* wakame, kombu, *hijiki, arame,* dulse, agar-agar, and Irish moss may be prepared in a variety of ways. They can be cooked with beans or vegetables, used in soups, or served separately as side dishes, flavored with a moderate amount of tamari soy sauce, sea salt, brown rice vinegar, *umeboshi* plum, umeboshi vinegar, and others.

5. Occasional foods. If needed or desired, one to three times a week, approximately 5 to 10 percent of that day's consumption of food can include fresh white-meat fish such as flounder, sole, cod, carp, halibut, or trout.

Fruit or fruit desserts, including fresh, dried, and cooked fruits, may also be served two or three times a week. Local and organically grown fruits are preferred. If you live in a temperate climate, avoid tropical and semi-tropical fruit and eat, instead, temperate-climate fruits such as apples, pears, plums, peaches, apricots, berries, and melons. Frequent use of fruit juice is not advisable. However, occasional consumption in warmer weather may be appropriate depending on your health.

Lightly roasted nuts and seeds such as pumpkin, sesame, and sunflower seeds, peanuts, walnuts, and pecans may be enjoyed as a snack.

Rice syrup, barley malt, *amazaké*, and *mirin* may be used as a sweetener; brown rice vinegar or umeboshi vinegar may be used occasionally for a sour taste.

6. Beverages. Recommended daily beverages include roasted *bancha* twig tea, stem tea, roasted brown rice tea, roasted barley tea, dandelion tea, and cereal grain coffee. Any traditional tea that does not have an aromatic fragrance or a stimulating effect can be used. You may also drink a moderate amount of water (preferably spring or well water of good quality) but not iced.

7. Foods to eliminate for better health. Meat, animal fat, eggs, poultry, dairy products (including butter, yogurt, ice cream, milk, and cheese), refined sugars, chocolate, molasses, honey, other simple sugars and foods treated with them, and vanilla.

Tropical and semi-tropical fruits and fruit juices, soda, artificial drinks and beverages, coffee, colored tea, and all aromatic, stimulating teas such as mint or peppermint tea.

All artificially colored, preserved, sprayed, or chemically treated foods; all refined and polished grains, flours, and their derivatives; mass-produced industrialized food including all canned, frozen, and irradiated foods.

Hot spices, any aromatic stimulating food or food accessory, artificial vinegar, and strong alcoholic beverages.

8. Additional suggestions. Cooking oil should be vegetable quality only. To improve your health, it is preferable to use only unrefined sesame or corn oil in moderate amounts.

Salt should be naturally processed sea salt. Traditional, non-chemicalized *shoyu* or tamari soy sauce and miso may also be used as seasonings.

Recommendable condiments include:
- *Gomashio* (twelve to eighteen parts roasted sesame seeds to one part roasted sea salt)
- Sea-vegetable powder (kelp, kombu, wakame, and other sea vegetables)
- Sesame sea vegetable powder
- Umeboshi plums
- *Tekka* condiment made from roasted, ground roots
- Tamari soy sauce or shoyu (moderate use, only in cooking for mild flavoring)
- Pickles (made using bran, miso, tamari soy sauce, salt), sauerkraut

You may have meals regularly, two to three times per day, as much as you want, provided the proportion is correct and chewing is thorough. Avoid eating for approximately three hours before sleeping.

The importance of cooking. Proper cooking is very important for health. Everyone should learn to cook either by attending classes or under the guidance of an experienced macrobiotic cook. The recipes included in macrobiotic cookbooks may also be used in planning your meals.

Special advice. The guidelines suggested above are general recommendations. They may require modification depending on your special condition. Of course, any serious condition should be closely monitored by the appropriate medical, nutritional, and health professional.

Way of Life Suggestions

- Live each day happily without being preoccupied with your health; try to keep mentally and physically active.
- View everything and everyone you meet with gratitude, particularly offering thanks before and after every meal.
- Please chew your food very well, at least fifty times per mouthful, or until it becomes liquid.
- It is best to retire before midnight and get up early every morning.
- It is best to avoid wearing synthetic or woolen clothing directly on the skin. As much as possible, wear cotton, especially for undergarments. Avoid excessive metallic accessories on the fingers, wrists, or neck. Keep such ornaments simple and graceful.
- If your strength permits, go outdoors in simple clothing. Walk on the grass, beach, or soil up to one half hour everyday. Keep your home in good order, from the kitchen, bathroom, bedroom, and living rooms, to every corner of the house.
- Initiate and maintain an active correspondence, extending your best wishes to parents, children, brothers and sisters, teachers, and friends.
- Avoid taking long hot baths or showers unless you have been consuming too much salt or animal food.
- To increase circulation, scrub your entire body with a hot, damp towel every morning or every night. If that is not possible, at least scrub your hands, feet, fingers, and toes.
- Avoid chemically perfumed cosmetics. For care of the teeth, brush with natural preparations or sea salt.
- If your condition permits, exercise regularly as part of daily life, including activities like walking, scrubbing floors, cleaning windows, washing clothes, and working in the garden. You may also participate in exercise programs such as yoga, martial arts, dance, or sports.
- Avoid using electric cooking devices (ovens and ranges) or microwave ovens. Convert to gas or wood-stove cooking at the earliest opportunity.
- It is best to minimize the use of color television and computer display units.
- Include some large green plants in your house to freshen and enrich the oxygen content of the air of your home.
- Sing a happy song everyday.

Chapter 2

We Are Energy

In ancient times, the arts of medicine were based on the understanding that human beings are made of energy. Long before electronic devices were invented to detect and measure energy flow, mankind had drawn maps of the pathways taken by energy as it flows through our body. These maps were the result of many years of experience, experimentation, and practice by the use of natural intuition and thought processes.

In China, the flow of *chi* (氣) was mapped through the meridian system and acupuncture points; in Japan, the presence of *ki* (氣) formed the foundation for arts such as Aikido, in which energy flow is emphasized in martial-art practice. In India, yogis and yoginis mastered the art of regulating *prana* through control of the breath. Ancient Egyptians revered the *ka* of a departed king. Native American healing customs revolved around mankind's role as part of the flow of nature, emanating from the Great Spirit; various words for energy existed according to the specific tribe. These terms all refer to energy, life-force, the universal mover of all things. In traditional cultures, mankind knew of the existence and importance of energy, and developed practices for maintaining and enhancing a healthy energy flow.

Fig. 2 : 1
Forces from the sky, including the sun, moon, stars and other particles in space, radiate energy upon the earth about 7 times greater than the force generated outward and upward by the rotation of the earth.

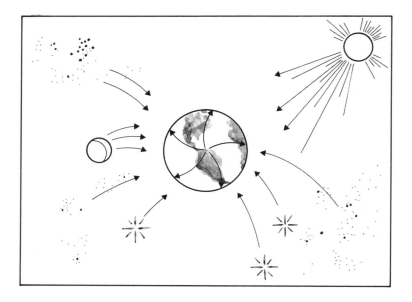

Fig. 2:2
Heaven's and Earth's forces in a landscape of mountains and valleys. Heaven's force, descending, creates the valleys; Earth's force, ascending, pushes up the mountains.

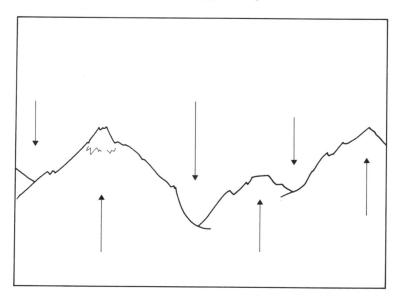

In the twentieth century, a number of researchers have discovered ways to measure and detect life energy using electric or magnetic machines. There is an electric acupuncture-point locator which detects the increased charge at the exact location of each point. Kirlian photography, a special photographic technique, captures pictures of the human aura or energy field, as well as the auras of plants and animals. Radionic devices detect and measure the rate of vibration of the life energy of a person or plant at a distance. These are just a few examples of the many such inventions that have been developed in this century.

All of these schools of thought agree that we are supported and sustained by an underlying flow of life energy. When this flow is impeded, we become weak or sick; when it stops, we pass away. When the flow of energy is strengthened and cared for, we become stronger and healthier.

Where does our energy come from? The universe is full of energy, alive with the flow of universal life-force. The scientific person thinks of it as an electric or magnetic force; the religious person thinks of it in terms of God. Energy radiates down to us from the sun, moon, and distant stars; it radiates up to us from the rotating force of the Earth. These forces of energy streaming down to us from Heaven (yang force) and up to us from the Earth (yin force) have been called the source of creation of everything in nature—all people, animals, plants, and inanimate objects. Fig. 2:1 illustrates Heaven's and Earth's forces operating upon our planet. Notice that the force from the sky is approximately seven times greater than that from the Earth.

Fig. 2:2 shows the influence of Heaven's and Earth's forces in a landscape of mountains and valleys.

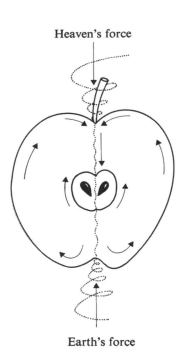

Heaven's force

Earth's force

Fig. 2:3
Heaven's and Earth's forces interact to form an apple.

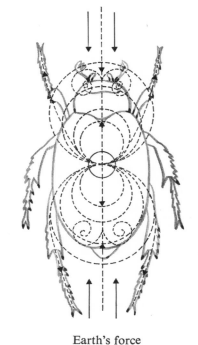

Heaven's force

Earth's force

Fig. 2:4
Heaven's and Earth's forces forming an insect, with a ratio of about 1:1.

The mountains are created by upward-flowing Earth's force, the valleys by downward-flowing Heaven's force.

The interaction of these upward and downward flows of energy produce the invisible structures of plants and animals in the embryonic form, which gather matter upon their forms and grow and unfold into materialized beings. Fig. 2:3 shows the energy formation of an apple, and Fig. 2:4 shows that of an insect, which receives Heaven's and Earth's forces in different proportion than the apple.

Fig. 2:5 shows how our human form results from the interaction of Heaven's and Earth's forces, with the force from the sky about seven times greater than that from the Earth.

Unlike the insect, the human form is larger in the lower half of the body, from

Fig. 2:5
Our human body, formed by Heaven's and
Earth's forces in a ratio of about 7:1.

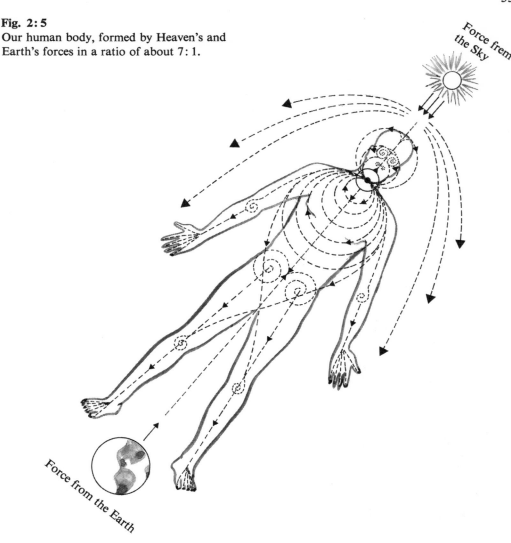

the neck down, due to the greater extension by Heaven's force. The upper part of
the body, the head, is smaller, being only about one-seventh the size of the whole
body; yet it is a miniature version of the lower body. Each organ in the lower body
has its compact replica in the head, as we will study further in Chapter 6.

Notice that the energy pathways move in spirals rather than straight lines, resulting in the rounded, spirallic structures of organic beings. In our human form,
the mouth is at the center of our total body spiral. These spirals result when the
forces of Heaven and Earth collide, deflecting each other into spirallic pathways.
This results in the formation of our internal organs and all other body structures.
The spiral at the top of the head is visible as a hair spiral and marks the spot
where the forces coming down from the sun and stars enter the top of our main
channel of energy flow. The spirals near the tips of our fingers and toes show where
energy flows outward to the environment.

Our Energy System

Energy constantly flows through our body, sustaining our life. Fig. 2: 6 shows the main channel of energy or *Spiritual channel* running down the center of our body, with Heaven's and Earth's forces spiralling to create it. The spiritual channel functions like a main power line carrying energy through the body as a whole. Along the spiritual channel are a number of *chakras*, as shown in Fig. 2: 6. The chakras are major energy centers of the body and may be compared to electrical transformers, each one gathering energy and distributing it in its locale, in the appropriate frequency. Seven major chakras are shown, each one having an important influence on the organs in the surrounding area. We will discuss them in more detail in Chapter 5.

Fig. 2: 6
The spiritual channel and the seven major chakras.

From the spiritual channel, meridians branch off carrying energy to all parts of the body. The meridians are not physical structures like blood vessels, but rather are pathways along which energy flows. There are twelve major meridians plus the Governing and Conception Vessels, each relating to the functions of a specific bodily organ or group of organs. Fig. 2: 7 shows an overview of our system of meridians, which are shown in detail in Chapter 7.

Along each meridian are many points (*tsubo*) which function as tiny holes allowing energy to enter and exit the meridian. Over 360 points are commonly recognized, and many are used in classical Oriental medicine for the treatment of disease. The meridians and points are used in acupuncture and shiatsu massage, and we can also utilize them in the art of palm healing, as described in Chapter 7.

Fig. 2:7
Overview of our meridian system

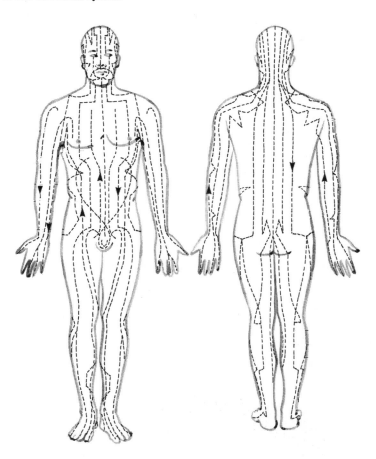

Visible and Invisible Food

Our body is nourished by physical food, assimilated by the digestive system, and by energy food, assimilated by our energy system—the chakras, spiritual channel, meridians, and points. In order to live, we need both kinds of food, and both systems must function well. We take care of our digestive system by eating good-quality food. We take care of our energy system by taking in good-quality energy. How do we make sure that we take in good-quality energy, and how do we avoid taking in bad-quality energy? The following list names some important ways.

- Cheerful, happy, positive thought patterns have a beneficial effect on our energy, while negative, pessimistic, depressing thoughts tend to deplete our energy.

- Eating good-quality physical food provides us with good energy through the energy structure of the foods themselves. Foods that are whole, natural, and fresh, are alive and brimming with energy, while those that are highly processed and refined have lost their vitality, and eating them requires an expenditure of energy.
- We energize ourselves through beneficial daily habits such as exercise, fresh air, and the proper amount of sleep. Poor health habits require an expenditure of energy to compensate for them and leave us in a tired condition.
- The frequent practice of palm healing, as both giver and receiver, contributes to our energy in a positive way.
- Other related practices such as Dō-In, shiatsu, yoga, and martial arts also contribute.
- Spiritual practices and meditation are very helpful.

The Aura

The aura is our energy field which surrounds and permeates our body. Not only human beings, but also animals, plants, and other living things have auras. Our human aura includes the spiritual channel, chakras, and meridian flow, all contributing to our total energy makeup. Fig. 2:8 illustrates the human aura.

Fig. 2:8
The aura: (A) Inner, (B) Middle, and (C) Outer layers. A more detailed study may reveal further divisions.

Notice that the aura extends beyond the solid physical body. The aura is more yin and expanded. It shows three general layers beyond the physical body. The inner, most dense part of the aura, sometimes called the *etheric body*, extends about one inch beyond the physical body. The next layer may extend several feet beyond the body and is even less dense; it is generally associated with our emotional experience. The third layer may extend many feet beyond the body and is very thin and fine; it is associated with our finer mental and spiritual experience.

The aura is not a fixed structure: the yin, expanded energy acts like a fluid, constantly moving, flowing, and changing. Our energy field changes from day to day, influenced by our daily activity, thoughts, diet, habits, climate, and environment. It even changes from one minute to the next depending upon what influences are affecting us.

We can build a strong, healthy aura able to resist negative influences and meet our demands for daily energy expenditure, through the beneficial diet and way-of-life practices already described. An energy field in such a good condition creates good physical and mental health. The practice of palm healing is also a contributing factor.

Within the aura, differences may be noticed from one spot to another. For example, someone might have a healthy energy field around the stomach, but show a weak or lower-quality energy condition near the heart. This may reflect existing conditions in the person's physical body. Since the energy flow underlies and causes our physical condition, these differences may indicate an energy pattern that is developing but has not yet manifested in the physical body. A person who can sense the aura can thus detect a sickness before it develops in the body, and take measures to prevent it.

Since our energy is constantly moving and changing, it would be nearly impossible to have a perfectly balanced aura at all times; usually we have some kind of imbalance. Through natural care, we can regulate our energy enough, however, to reduce extreme imbalances, and experience fewer major fluctuations from one extreme to the other. A healthy energy field is strong, even, and steadily radiating in all areas. Physical and mental health naturally follows.

Detecting the Aura

We have seen that there are a number of modern inventions, such as Kirlian photography, that are able to detect the aura through electrical or magnetic, mechanical means. People can also learn to detect the aura without any mechanical assistance, just by the use of our senses. This may require some practice and training, and it is very helpful to develop good health and a clear mind through appropriate diet and lifestyle in order to do this.

Depending on the person, the perception of energy in the aura may take place in several ways:

Kinesthetic sense.   Have you ever sensed someone's presence in a room even though you did not see that person, and no sounds were made? This is an example of the kinesthetic sense. It is as though we were sensing someone's energy in a general way, perhaps with our whole body. This is not surprising when we remember that energy, although usually invisible, is still real and has physical properties, although more expanded and light than dense matter. It may be possible that our large, extended aura encountered the large, extended aura of the other person entering the room.

Touch.   As we develop greater awareness, our ability to detect energy through touch increases. Holding the palms of the hands near the aura, we feel various sensations of heat, coolness, electricity, or magnetism. The practice of palm healing assists in the development of this sense.

Sight.   Many people have reported seeing the aura as though with an inner sight. The energy field can be quite beautiful, with colors that change from one area to another, reflecting changes in the physical and emotional condition.

Hearing.   Some people who are quite sensitive to sound develop the ability to hear the aura. The energy field is interpreted as a series of musical tones or as a single tone which differs from person to person.

Smell.   It has been reported that certain people sense someone else's aura as a characteristic smell, even when the person is so far distant that physical smelling is not possible. They have developed the ability to interpret the vibrations caused by the energy field as smell.

These seemingly remarkable abilities are not so strange when we consider that they have been developed through practice, awareness, and attention over a considerable period of time. Most of us simply do not spend a large amount of time thinking about the aura or noticing energy. But if we choose to do so, we find that is not too difficult to develop the awareness of energy through touch, or perhaps through sight, or one of the other means. Then it can become an invaluable aid in determining our health condition or that of another person, for the purpose of improving health and happiness.

If we improve our own health condition through a good-quality diet and lifestyle, our awareness and alertness automatically increases and our ability to perceive energy and the aura becomes commonplace. At the same time, we develop qualities of cheerfulness and optimism that contribute to our effectiveness as a healer. If we wish to receive palm healing care from someone else, it is best to choose a person who has these same qualities.

The energy system is an important part of the whole human being. In order to practice wholistic healing, care and attention for the energy system is of great importance. The practice of giving and receiving palm healing is very helpful. Through the macrobiotic approach, we can learn to do this in the most balanced and effective way.

Fig. 2: 9 is an artistic representation of our human energy system, including the spiritual channel, chakras, meridians and aura. For the purpose of study, we can analyze each part separately, but in reality, they operate as a unit. This is one of the universe's remarkable phenomena, the human energy system—living, moving, radiating—a source of joyful life.

Fig. 2: 9
The human energy system, a moving and radiating source of life.

Chapter 3

Foundations of Palm Healing

The process of learning how to practice palm healing begins with the simple elements needed to encourage a good energy flow—personal care and attitude, sitting positions, methods of breathing, ways of using the hands, and some simple sounds that can be chanted. These form the foundation of a good practice of palm healing.

Personal Care and Attitude

Since the condition of the healer is so important for success in palm healing, we recommend the healthful macrobiotic diet and lifestyle outlined in Chapter 1 as one of the foundations of palm healing. The following points can be added and emphasized as well.

Diet
- Choose whole foods which contain complete energy, rather than foods which have been processed, refined, or otherwise broken up. For example, choose radishes with their leaves still on and eat the entire plant.
- Minimize animal foods, sweets, fats, and excess liquid. Emphasize whole grains, vegetables, beans, and sea vegetables.
- An excessive liquid intake results in moist palms which inhibit energy flow in palm healing. Similar effects are obtained from eating excessive oil, even good-quality oil, and too much raw vegetables or fruit, which contain plenty of liquid.
- It is better to practice palm healing one hour or more after eating a meal, rather than right away.
- Chew every mouthful very well, at least fifty times or more.
- Do not eat until very ful. Allow a little space to remain in the stomach after eating (about 2/3 full). Do not eat late at night just before sleeping. Allow two to three hours to elapse before sleep.

Activity
- Be aware of your posture and do not slump while sitting or standing. A good posture allows energy to flow well through the spiritual channel.
- Maintain a good level of physical activity if possible.
- Try to get some outdoor exercise or fresh air, and some exposure to nature; even a few minutes is helpful. We pick up energy from nature.
- While walking outside, swing your hands vigorously to generate energy movement in and out of the body.

Clothing
- Emphasize natural-fiber clothing in designs that fit loosely without constricting the circulation of blood, energy, and air.
- Accessories such as belts, necklaces, and bracelets can be lightweight, natural materials such as cotton, macrame, straw, wood, shell, and so on. Remove your watch or metal accessories during palm healing.
- Avoid using chemically made lotion, nail polish, and other cosmetics, substituting natural items.

Environment
- Fresh, clean air and sunlight in the home bring in natural energy.
- Green plants replenish the supply of oxygen.
- Choose normal (incandescent) light bulbs or other natural types of lighting in the home, rather than neon and flourescent lights.
- Choose wood, straw, cotton, and other natural materials in the home instead of synthetics.
- Avoid the use of too many electrical appliances. Turn them off and unplug them when possible to reduce the amount of residual electric flow in the environment.
- Create a peaceful, pleasant environment with appealing colors and decor, and reduce unnecessary noise for a peaceful atmosphere.
- If practicing palm healing on an unnatural surface such as a concrete or vinyl floor, bring in a block of wood to rest your other hand on, and sit on a cotton cushion, or other natural covering.

Attitude
- Be cheerful, happy, optimistic. Create good feelings.
- Study some spiritual or mental discipline. Learn how to use the mind to help produce good health.
- Always be grateful for your daily life, for the universe. Respect and love all humanity and the wonders of nature.
- Have a positive wish to heal, to see other people become healthy.
- Do not think "I am the healer"; rather, think "I am an agent or channel through which healing is taking place." Recognize that the true healer is the universal energy, or God, and not the personal ego.

Is It Always Safe to Use Palm Healing?
Since palm healing is a gentle practice with practically no side effects, it is a very safe practice to use under most circumstances. In deciding whether or not to use palm healing for a specific person, the following points should be considered:

1. *Does the person wish it?* Most people will request palm healing, but if someone does not wish it—due to illness, oversensitivity, or simple preference—then do not insist. Instead, you may use distant healing as described in Chapter 11.
2. *Is the person very ill or oversensitive?* If someone is interested in receiving

palm healing but is very weak, ill or hypersensitive, it is important to give an especially careful, gentle application, and if discomfort develops, stop or take a rest. Unless you have considerable experience, it may be best to use

simple exercises to calm, generate energy, and balance rather than lengthy specialized exercises for such persons.

3. *Are you practicing a balanced pattern?* A palm healing session that follows the recommended sequence including preparation, balancing, and closing exercises, will result in a balanced feeling.

Using the Hands

The centers of the palms function as important, secondary chakras or energy centers of the body. When doing palm healing, this central palm chakra is placed over the area needing care. (See Fig. 3: 1).

Near the tip of each finger and thumb are spirals which indicate points of strong energy flow. In certain exercises which use a single finger or thumb instead of the entire palm, it is this spiral point which touches the area needing care. Note that this is not the tip of the finger but more the pad, as shown in Fig. 3: 1.

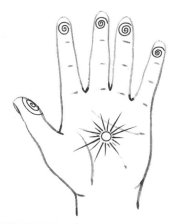

Fig. 3: 1
Central palm chakra, finger and thumb spirals.

Of all the areas on the hands, the center of the palm is the most powerful and effective in palm healing. Next, the thumb, then, the long middle finger, then the index finger, finally the fourth and little fingers.

When giving palm healing, the fingers should not be widely spread —which causes a scattering of energy—but should be held fairly close together in a relaxed way, with perhaps a fraction-of-an-inch space between them.

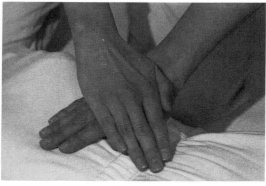

1 Practicing palm healing

The palms should be fairly dry and cool, not too moist or too warm. The condition of the palm is a result of our daily diet and habits. During palm healing the receiver may sometimes feel a sensation of warmth coming from the giver's hands, but this is different from a prior condition of warm, sticky hands, which indicates an excess in the diet of liquid, oil, fats, sweets, and/or raw foods.

Right hand or left?   In general, we recommend using your dominant or strongest hand to give palm healing. If you are right-handed, use your right hand in the most important healing positions. If left-handed, use your left. In Chapter 8 we will discuss additional considerations of which hand to use for certain purposes.

One hand or both?   Palm healing may be done with one hand, or with two. When using one hand, the other can rest in the lap, or can be held up in the air as if gathering in Heaven's force, or down toward the ground as if gathering in Earth's force (Fig. 3:2). When using two hands, do not place them on top of each other, as the left and right hands tend to cancel out or neutralize each other's energy. Instead, use the hands in different positions in a complementary fashion, as included in a number of exercises in the book.

Do not "leak" energy by unintentionally touching the receiver in some part of the body other than that which you intend to work on. Sit so that your feet, elbows, other hand, and so on do not touch the receiver. This may cause an unintentional deflection of energy. Touch only the intended spot with the intended hand.

Which direction should we face?   In the Northern Hemisphere, if we face south while giving palm healing, we have the benefit of the stream of energy flowing down from the north pole entering our backs and adding power to our healing efforts. In the morning, we can face southwest so that both the northern sky and the sun rising in the east are at our backs. In the evening, we can face southeast so that the northern sky and the power of the setting sun in the west are entering our backs (Fig. 3:3). In the Southern Hemisphere, our backs should be to the south pole from which energy pours toward the equator, so we can substitute "south" for "north" in the above recommendations.

Of course, it is alright to face any direction, but the above suggestions give the maximum results for healing energy.

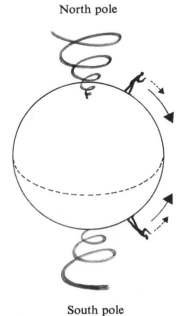

North pole

South pole

Fig. 3:2
Energy flowing from the poles toward the Equator can be harnessed for palm healing.

Fig. 3:3

We can maximize our energy during palm healing by facing different directions at different times to make use of the power of the sun as well as the energy coming from the poles. This diagram shows the directions from which maximum energy is coming at different times of day in each hemisphere. We can sit with our back to these directions so that these stronger energies may enter our backs and be projected forward during palm healing. For example, in the northern hemisphere in the morning, with our back to the northeast we pick up the energy of the sun rising in the east, as well as the energy flowing down from the north pole.

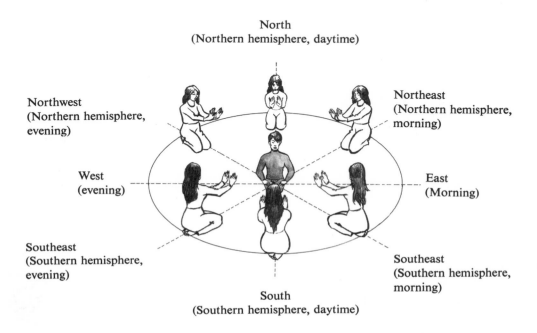

North
(Northern hemisphere, daytime)

Northwest
(Northern hemisphere, evening)

Northeast
(Northern hemisphere, morning)

West
(evening)

East
(Morning)

Southeast
(Southern hemisphere, evening)

Southeast
(Southern hemisphere, morning)

South
(Southern hemisphere, daytime)

Sitting Positions

While giving or receiving palm healing, we should maintain a posture that is straight enough for energy to flow up and down the spiritual channel well, but relaxed enough so that we feel comfortable and flexible rather than rigid or tense. The following positions are suitable for this purpose and we will refer to them throughout the exercises that follow. Often we recommend the *Seiza* posture, but the others are suitable as well depending on your preference.

When sitting with good posture, we feel as though we are floating, and as though we are pulled up at the top of our head with a cord, rather than feeling that we are "holding ourselves up."

If sitting on the floor, a comfortable cotton cushion or *zabuton* is recommended for both giver and receiver.

1. Seiza Posture. This traditional meditation posture gives a springiness to our

2

3

Pauline demonstrates the seiza posture

Seiza posture, back view

spine and a lift to our whole body. We kneel with the knees separated about the width of one fist. The buttocks rest on the soles of the feet. The toes are slightly overlapped. Tradition holds that if your legs become cramped in this position, just uncross your toes and cross them again with the other foot on top to refresh your circulation.

2. Half-Lotus Posture. This is another traditional meditation posture. The legs are crossed, but one foot rests on the opsite thigh, while the other foot is underneath the other thigh. Sometimes an extra cushion is folded and placed under the buttocks for support.

3. Lotus Posture. This traditional meditation posture requires flexibility in the legs and some people find it difficult. If it

4

Half-lotus posture demonstrated by Lillian (left): Lotus posture demonstrated by Diane (right)

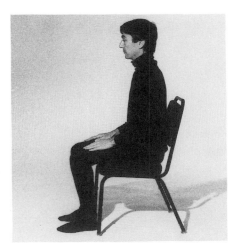

5 Steve demonstrates palm healing posture on a chair.

can be done without strain, it is a good position for posture. The legs are crossed, and each foot is placed on top of the opposite thigh. As for the half-lotus posture, an extra cushion may be placed under the buttocks for support if needed.

4. Sitting on a Chair. This is also a good posture for palm healing, especially when the floor postures feel uncomfortable. The buttocks and small of the back should be resting against the back of the chair to encourage good carriage. Feet are on the floor, pointing generally straight ahead, but in a relaxed fashion.

Hand Positions

The way we hold our hands affects the way energy flows through our body. The following hand positions are recommended for various purposes during palm healing practice, and will be referred to throughout the exercises.

1. Peaceful Position. This hand position is conducive to a feeling of calm, receptive peacefulness. The hands rest palm upward in the lap, the left hand on top, the right hand underneath. The tips of the thumbs touch lightly.

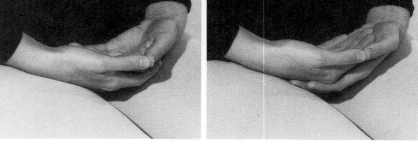

6   1. Peaceful position   7   2. Activating position

2. Activating Position. The energy flow created by this position leads to an active, alert feeling. It is similar to the Peaceful Position, but the right hand is now on top, the left hand underneath.

8   3. Unifying position

9   3. Unifying position with elbows up

3. Unifying Position. This position connects our right and left side body energies, resulting in a feeling of wholeness and unification. It is also known as the Prayer Position. The hands are held palms together in front of the chest, touching lightly without effort. Fingers are not spread widely apart but are fairly close together, in a relaxed fashion. If it is comfortable to do so, in this position the elbows can be raised so that the forearms are parallel to the floor, palms held together in the same relaxed manner. This improves posture and increases energy flow.

4. Secure Position. The hands are folded in the lap. This serves to connect our right and left side energy flow, and has a yang influence, giving a feeling of harmonizing and holding energy inside. Warmth and inner reflection result. Try this position first with one thumb on top, then the other, noticing the difference.

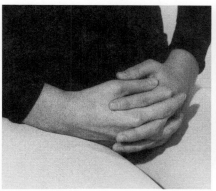

10   4. Secure position

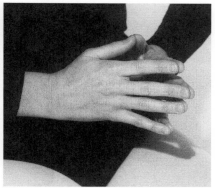

11   5. Stabilizing position

5. Stabilizing Position. The hands are held so that the tips of all fingers and thumbs are touching those of the opposite hand. Fingers are just slightly spread and hands rest in the lap. This position unites our right and left energy flow, giving a feeling of harmony and the finger positions create a feeling of stability and balance.

6. Focusing Position. Hands resting in the lap, the right thumb and index finger touch the tips of the left thumb and index finger. The remaining fingers are folded. This creates a yang influence helpful for focused, well-directed thought.

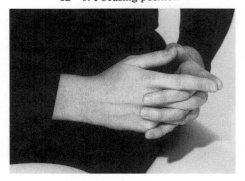

12   6. Focusing position

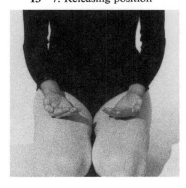

13   7. Releasing position

7. Releasing Position. The hands rest palm-up on the thighs. Thumb and index finger may touch to form a circle, or may simply rest open. This open, relaxed, yin position is helpful for releasing tension and tightness which has been held inside, and for developing a feeling of generosity,

50

as well as receptivity. Physical lightness and coolness are also created.

8. Receiving Heaven's Force. Hands are raised toward the sky, at about shoulder level, lightly opened to pick up energy coming down from the sky. Notice that to pick up yang Heaven's force, we hold our hands in an upward, yin posture. Raising the hands higher, above shoulder level, increases the amount of yang force coming in.

8. Receiving Heaven's force   9. Receiving Earth's force

16 10. Receiving both Heaven's and Earth's force

9. Receiving Earth's Force. Hands are extended toward the Earth, held lightly open in a flexible manner to receive the energy coming up from the Earth.

10. Receiving Both Heaven's and Earth's Force. One hand is held up, the other down, to receive energy from both Heaven and Earth. Try both hands in each position, but generally the right hand, which has a stronger flow of Earth's force, may be raised to attract more Heaven's force, and vice versa.

Methods of Breathing

Often we are not aware of our breathing, yet it is one of our most important actions. Through breathing we bring oxygen into the body, regenerating our blood supply, and we discharge gaseous wastes from the body. At the same time, our breath helps to control the in-and-out flow of Heaven's and Earth's force, bringing in new energy and discharging stagnation. Our manner of breathing is essential in regulating our energy flow as well as our physical, mental and emotional condition, and it is an important factor in palm healing. Some basic methods of regulating our breathing follow.[1]

1.   Natural Breathing.   Sitting comfortably with good posture, allow the breathing to fall into its own natural rhythm. Let the mind be peaceful and do not let anything disturb the breathing. Do not try to make the breathing follow any particular pattern, but allow it to become very smooth and comfortable, moving in and out regularly. This type of breathing puts us in a peaceful, balanced state of body and mind.

2.   Full Breathing.   This method may be used from time to time to bring in extra energy and power. It is done in a smooth, regular movement, but we have broken it down into steps for easy comprehension:
   a.   As we begin the breath, let the air first fill the bottom of the lungs. As this happens, the abdomen expands.
   b.   As we continue, we allow air to fill the middle part of the lungs, expanding the central area of the body.
   c.   Finally the chest expands as the top of the lungs is filled.
   d.   Hold the breath for a few seconds.
   e.   To breathe out, reverse the process. First empty the top of the chest, then the middle, then the abdomen (bottom of the lungs).
   f.   Sit empty for a few seconds, then begin the next breath.
   Do not strain in practicing this breath, but breathe in a smooth, comfortable manner. We can check whether the abdomen is expanding by placing one hand there and noticing if it rises and falls with the inhalation and exhalation.

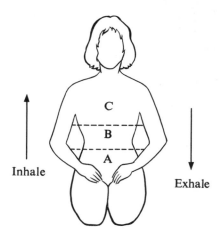

During Full Breathing, we first breathe into area "A," then "B," then "C." To exhale, reverse the process: empty "C," then "B," then "A."

3.   Yin Breathing.   This method of breathing utilizes yin factors of upward motion, slow speed, and expansion to produce an effect of coolness, relaxation, lightness,

---

[1] For a more detailed study of breathing, see *The Book of Dō-In* by Michio Kushi.

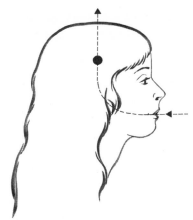

In Yin Breathing, the air enters the lungs as usual, but our *intention* causes the *energy* of the breath to move upward, as shown.

and spiritualization or detachment from the environment. It is helpful when we feel too yang—hot, tense, hurried. If someone feels too yin—cold, light-headed or depressed—this type of breathing should only be done for a very short time, or not at all.

Sitting with hands in the Releasing Position, we breathe in a slow, unhurried manner. The inhalation, which is more yin, can be two to three times longer than the exhalation. Breathe in an upward direction, emphasizing expansion in the upper body rather than the abdomen. We feel as though the breath is moving upward toward the top of the head. Hold the breath for a few seconds, then slowly breathe out. Continue this exercise, breathing in to the count of ten or fifteen, and breathing out to the count of five, for several minutes.

4. Yang Breathing. This method encourages a feeling of warmth, activity, solidity, and stability upon the earth. It is very helpful in cold weather, or for someone who feels overly yin—cold, indecisive, insecure. A person who feels too yang may not enjoy this exercise. Yang breathing utilizes the yangizing factors of downward motion, faster speed, and contraction.

The hands may be held in the Activating Position, Secure Position, or another position that tends toward a yang effect. This time, the exhalation is longer than

In Yang Breathing, our intention while breathing creates a downward energy flow.

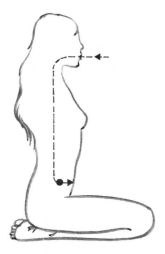

the inhalation, emphasizing the yang force of contraction, and a faster breathing speed can be used. The downward motion is emphasized by concentrating on breathing down into the abdominal region.

Breathe in to the count of two, hold the breath for a few seconds, then breathe out to the count of five or seven. After breathing out, pause for a few seconds experiencing the effects of contraction, before beginning the next inhalation. Continue for two to three minutes.

The Use of Sound

Sound creates a vibration which influences our energy. There are many sounds and many ways to utilize them in meditation and in palm healing. Certain sounds can be chanted or sung to activate our energy, to harmonize energy, or to calm our energy. In Chapter 8 we will discuss sound in more detail. Following are some basic sounds which can be used often during palm healing.

Su.   Pronounced "Sue," this is a balanced sound which creates an energy vibration to harmonize our energy. We can chant "Su" in a long, peaceful manner to create a smooth, calm feeling. This sound helps to regulate energy flow in general and produces a feeling of unification, drawing all extremes to the middle. Repeat about five to ten times in a long, slow manner to feel the effect of this sound.

Ah.   This is a yin, open sound which produces an effect of releasing and relaxation. It may be chanted slowly five to ten times to see the effect.

Toh.   Pronounced "Toe," this is a yang, concentrated sound, useful for activating and focusing our energy and creating a feeling of warmth. "Toh" may be chanted in a more short, active manner.

Mmm.   A very closed, contracted sound, "Mmm" gives a yang effect and is helpful for focusing and concentration, especially in the mind.

A-U-M.   Many people are familiar with this sound, "Aum" or "Om," which is practiced by ancient religions. For the fullest effect, we pronounce it as three separate sounds, "Ah-U-Mmm." These three sounds represent yin, middle, and yang sounds, and give us a very energizing effect, and a feeling of wholeness or completeness, together with a sense of universal consciousness. "A-U-M" is chanted in one long breath, giving about equal time to each sound. Try it about ten times or two to three minutes.

Types of Meditation

Meditation is an important practice to regulate our mind and energy flow. It is used in preparation for palm healing, both for the giver and the receiver. Many styles of meditation exist, some using more yin factors, some more yang factors. We may choose the type that is needed for each specific situation. Following are three basic styles of meditation, which are useful to know for our practice of palm healing.[2]

---

[2] For a further study of meditation, see *The Book of Dō-In* by Michio Kushi.

17   1. Basic meditation

1.   Basic Meditation.   This is a balanced form of meditation which helps to harmonize our energy and calm the mind. Sitting comfortably with good posture, we place the hands in the Peaceful Position (or a similarly balanced, peaceful position). Eyes can be closed, or slightly open, looking in a somewhat downward direction. We use gentle, Natural Breathing and allow the mind to rest in an empty state, or perhaps just noticing the sensations of breathing. Spending several minutes, we become increasingly peaceful and clear-headed. Our energy flow becomes calm, even, and harmonized.

18   2. Yin meditation

2.   Yin Meditation.   When we feel hot, hurried and tense, yin meditation can help. It produces a feeling of coolness, slowness, lightness and expansion. This style of meditation developed in hot climates such as southern India. It has a very spiritual emphasis, taking our attention away from worldly affairs, and away from our physical existence. Thus it is not particularly beneficial for people who are already too yin, who have a need to pull themselves "down to earth." Since even people who are more yin sometimes experience feeling too yang, however, everyone can benefit from yin meditation at some time.

Sitting with good posture, we place our hands in the Releasing Position, arms at the sides, palms turned forward and outward. The head faces forward with a slight upward tilt at the chin and the eyes look up as though at an object far above our heads. The mouth may be slightly open. We utilize yin breathing, as described earlier, the direction of breath going upward, and the inhalation longer than the exhalation. On the long, full inhalation, we may sway slightly forward and on the shorter exhalation, returning to the original position. Continue two to three minutes, noticing the feeling of lightness and coolness that develops. Do not continue if a feeling of light-headedness occurs.

3.   Yang Meditation.   This style of meditation gives us a feeling of warmth, stability, activity, and alertness. We feel very connected to the earth and our physical existence and we feel a sense of security. Yang Meditation is useful for adjusting to cold weather. Zen meditation, which developed in a northern climate, reflects these characteristics. Someone who feels too yin—cold, insecure, indecisive, passive—will benefit from this type of meditation.

19 3. Yang meditation

Our hands may be folded in the Secure Position or in the Activating Position, or another yang-oriented posture. The eyes may be closed or slightly open, looking down. The mouth remains closed. Yang breathing is used, emphasizing the downward motion toward the abdomen. The exhalation is longer than the inhalation. We may add a yang sound, if desired, such as "Toh" on the exhalation. Continue for several minutes, noticing the feeling of increasing warmth and security. We feel prepared for activity upon the earth.

Study Suggestion

Before going on to the next chapter, spend some time learning and practicing the hand positions, sitting postures, breathing methods, sounds, and meditations described in Chapter 3. Practice them in a relaxed, unhurried fashion in order to become familiar with each one. Once you feel comfortable with these basic practices, it will be much easier to practice the palm healing exercises described in subsequent chapters.

Chapter 4
The Order of Palm Healing

The purpose of palm healing is to increase our enjoyment of life. Some people like to emphasize the health-care aspect of palm healing, others are more interested in the way it educates us to the workings of energy, and still others appreciate it simply as a way to relax, reduce stress, or gain energy. Whatever approach is taken, please enjoy it with a smile! Have fun practicing palm healing and raising your level of health, happiness, and aliveness.

There are many possible ways to practice palm healing. We would like to recommend the pattern presented in this chapter as a simple, orderly, and effective way to proceed. It is designed to meet the basic needs for energy care and promote a feeling of balanced well-being. At the same time, it allows for the inclusion of variations or extra practices that may be needed by individuals. The outline below describes the steps in our recommended pattern of palm healing. In this chapter, each step will be described in detail.

I.   Preparation for the Giver
      A.   Calming the Mind with Meditation
      B.   Clearing the Aura
      C.   Generating Healing Ability
II.   Preparation for the Receiver
      A.   Calming the Mind with Meditation
      B.   Checking the Aura
      C.   Clearing the Aura
III.   Harmonizing the Whole Body's Energy Flow
IV.   Exercises for Special Purposes
V.   Finalization
      A.   Checking the Aura
      B.   Clearing the Aura
      C.   Stabilization
      D.   Rest

For each step, a number of different exercises may be practiced. We have included a selection under each category, from which you may choose one or more according to your needs.

The entire pattern is helpful for practicing a well-rounded, complete session of palm healing, so it is recommended to practice each step without leaving out any phase of the pattern.

In the beginning, extra time may be needed in order to learn each exercise, just as a cook requires extra time when preparing a new recipe for the first time. You may not notice remarkable results at first, either. But do not be discouraged. The value of palm healing lies partly in doing and experiencing, and in seeing how you progress from one month to the next, as both giver and receiver, and most of all, to learn, grow, and enjoy through the practice.

Preparation for the Giver

Before beginning, the person giving palm healing should take steps to clarify and strengthen his or her own energy flow. It is best if the giver has a condition that is better than, or at least equal to, that of the receiver. One way to ensure this is to follow a good-quality macrobiotic diet and lifestyle as we have already discussed. (In that sense, the preparation can be said to begin days, weeks, or even years in advance!) In any case, these preparatory exercises that follow can be done as a regular practice.

Remove metal jewelry, check the room for fresh air and open a window if needed. Arrange cushions and perhaps a chair. If desired, stretch or do a few minutes of Dō-In to limber up. You may want to remove your shoes and loosen the cuffs and collar if they are constrictive.

A.   Calming the Mind with Meditation.   We use meditation to bring our mind and energy flow to a state of calmness, clearness, and peacefulness. Use the meditation exercise described in Chapter 3, and spend several extra minutes if you have just come from a very busy, noisy environment that has affected your state of mind. Continue meditation until a feeling of peacefulness, calmness, and happiness is produced. Some people like to simply let the mind rest in an empty state, others like to have the assistance of pleasant meditational music or visualization.

1   1a. Beginning posture

In visualization, we create mental images that lead to an improvement in our energy state. For example, with eyes closed, we might imagine that we are in a lovely forest next to a lake. We mentally recreate the breeze passing through the trees, the sound of the waves gently lapping, the fragrance of nearby flowers. It is as though we can draw natural energy from these imaginary scenes.

B.   Clearing the Aura.   Our energy is affected by many influences—diet, activity, noise, encounters with other people, and the environment. Not all of these influences are beneficial, and residual effects from them may remain in the aura for some time afterward. This stagnation in the aura can obstruct our efforts to give palm healing and can affect our general condition of health. Consequently, we prac-

58

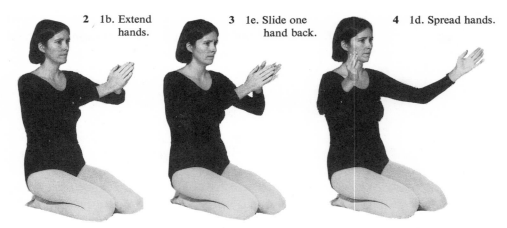

2 1b. Extend hands.

3 1e. Slide one hand back.

4 1d. Spread hands.

5 1e. Clap.

tice exercises designed to clear stagnation from the energy field. Two examples follow.

1. Simple Aura Clearing

   a. Sit in the Seiza or other sitting position, hands raised in the Unifying Position, palms held lightly together.

   b. Extend the hands forward, palms still held together.

   c. Slide one hand 1/2 to 1 inch back along the other, to create a clapping surface.

   d. Spread the hands wide apart.

   e. Clap sharply two times and allow a slight pause between claps while you spread the hands wide again. The claps should be sharp and brisk, as if to clear the air.

6 1g. Lower hands to thinghs.

7 1g. Form triangle.

8 1h. Bow.

   f. Repeat steps *d* and *e*.

   g. Lower the hands to the sides of the thighs and slide them down the legs to the floor in front, forming a triangle with the thumbs and index finger touching.

   h. Bow low, so that the nose goes down toward the middle of the triangle, but does not quite touch the floor.

9 1i. Sit up.

i. Sit up again and meditate peacefully. If desired, chant "Su" three to five times in long, peaceful breaths, hands in the Unifying Position.

j. Relax the hands in the lap and sit peacefully for a moment.

The sharp sound vibrations of the clapping help to break up and disperse stagnated energy. As we bow in step *h*, we form a complete circuit of our energy flow as well as stimulate the digestion system. At the same time, the bow symbolizes that we dedicate ourselves to the process of healing, and submit our egos to the greater wisdom of the infinite, universal life-force.

2. Aura Clearing by Clapping Five Times. A series of clapping motions is used to create sharp sound vibrations that disperse stagnated energy. These claps can be done in a rhythmic, musical manner if you wish.

a. Take the Seiza or other sitting position. Bring the hands to the Unifying Position in front of the chest.

b. Practice the following series of claps:
   • Clap two times to the front
   • Clap two times to the left
   • Clap two times to the front
   • Clap two times to the right
   Repeat this series five times, ending with two final claps to the front.

c. Slide your hands down the sides of the legs and bow as described in the first exercise.

10 2a. Beginning posture

11 2b. Clap in front.

12 2b. Clap left.

13 2b. Clap right.

14 2b. Clap front again.

15 2c. Slide hands down thighs.

60

d. Sit up again, chant "Su"
    several times, and finish with
    a few minutes of peaceful
    meditation.

16   2c. Bow.

17   2d. Sit up.

C. Generating Healing Ability. Certain exercises can serve to increase the flow of healing energy and direct it through our hands. Some examples follow. (We will introduce variations for two or more persons in Chapter 11.) These exercises are most effective when Meditation and Clearing the Aura Practice have been done first, setting up a clean, clear energy state in which healing energy can naturally increase.

In Generating Healing Ability, energy flowing through our body is increased and channeled to the hands for greater effectiveness in palm healing.

1. Generating Healing Ability: Basic Exercise

a. Sitting in the Seiza or other position, we place the hands in the Unifying Position in front of the chest, and breathe naturally, peacefully, and fully. Eyes may be closed or half open.

b. Continuing in this position, you may begin to feel heat, tingling, or vibration in the hands. The energy flow in the hands increases in this position, which acts much like charging a battery. Notice how your hands feel.

18

19

Generating healing ability with simple Unifying Position

Generating healing ability, hands slightly separated

c. Continue in the exercise several minutes until you feel a strong energy flow through the palms; then lower the hands to the lap and relax.

You may not notice any hand sensations the first few times you try this exercise, but after practicing several times this can occur. In any case, energy flow is definitely taking place.

2. Generating Healing Ability: Variations and Helpful Hints. The following practices may be used to increase energy, add variety and encourage experimentation while generating healing ability. Try adding one or more of these to the basic exercise that was just described, during step *b*.

20

a. Instead of touching the palms together, draw them slightly apart, perhaps 1/4 to 1/2 inch. Notice the feeling of energy flow even though the palms are not touching.

b. With the palms held slightly apart, rotate them in a forward-moving circle, one palm going up when the other goes down. How does it feel? Then, reverse the motion and notice the difference.

c. Touch the palms together, then slowly pull them several inches apart, and then slowly bring them back together again. Try this several times, noticing at what points you feel sensations of magnetism or energy.

d. Chant sounds to increase energy flow, such as "Su" or "A-U-M."

2e. Generating healing ability, thumbs touching throat

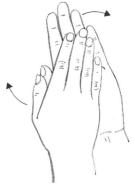

e. With the palms held together, bring the hands toward the throat and lightly touch the tips of the thumbs to the Adam's apple region. Breathe fully and naturally, adding the force of this energy center to that of the hands. Then, add chanting.

f. Holding the palms together near the mouth, blow across the tips of the fingers in a long stream of air as though forming the sound "whoooooo." This helps to dissipate stagnated energy at the fingertips and encourage the flow of healing energy.

g. Hold the palms up to receive Heaven's force, or down to receive Earth's force, or one up and one down as described in Chapter 3.

Step *b*: Rotate the palms one way, then the other for different energy effects.

h. Rub the palms together briskly to increase circulation of both blood and energy.

i. Add mental imagery—for example, picture a stream of light entering the top of your head, flowing down the arms and out through the hands.

3. Refreshing the Palms During Healing. While practicing palm healing, it sometimes happens that our hands become tired. It may be that we simply need a rest, or it may be that we have picked up some stagnated energy on our hands. When this happens, one of the following steps may be taken to refresh the palms. Then we can return to our practice.

Step *f*: Mentally visualizing a strong energy flow can assist in refreshing your energy during palm healing.

a. Rub the palms together briskly.
b. Rinse the hands under cold water.
c. Shake the hands briskly.
d. Brush the hand front and back.
e. Perform one of the clapping exercises.
f. Mentally visualize fresh, healing energy streaming into your body, down the arms and out the hands.
g. Refresh your circulation of energy by full, natural breathing.
h. Adjust your posture if you are not sitting in a straight but relaxed position.

Preparation for the Receiver

The person receiving palm healing care will obtain the best results by preparing himself or herself in much the same way that the healer does. A good diet and lifestyle are most helpful, and loose, comfortable, natural fiber clothing is best. Shoes and metal accessories can be removed, unless of course one does not wish to remove a wedding ring. If the receiving person also understands what palm healing is, he or she can participate in a relaxed, confident frame of mind.

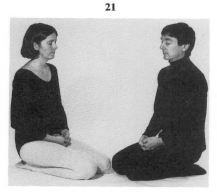

21

A. Giver and receiver meditating together

A. Calming the Mind with Meditation. To prepare for palm healing care, the receiving person can relax and meditate in the same way the healer does; refer to the first part of *Preparation for the Giver* for a description. He or she may meditate alone, or the giver may guide the receiver through the meditation. If desired, the two persons may also meditate together, which has the added benefit of harmonizing or attuning their energies.

B. Checking the Aura of the Receiver. The person giving palm healing care can become familiar with the receiver's energy flow by checking the aura. This is helpful in determining what kind of palm healing exercises to do. Persons receiving palm healing often report that this initial checking of the aura helps them to relax and get accustomed to palm healing as well.

The ability to sense the aura develops with practice, and we do not meet with success every time. Some people are able to do this right away, while others may need several practice sessions before feeling confident. In any case, it is beneficial to practice this step and sense the aura to the extent we can, at the same time exercising our abilities and giving some benefit to the receiver.

1. Aura-Sensing Exercise
a. The receiver sits comfortably with good posture, hands in the lap; eyes may be closed or gently open, and breathing is natural and peaceful.

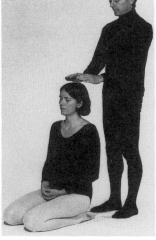 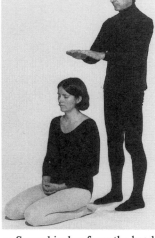

b. Checking the head area   c. Several inches from the head

b. The giver sits or stands at the back, the palms of the hands held several inches from the back of the head. Slowly, gently move the palms toward the receiver's head until they are about 2 inches away. Do you feel a magnetic or electrical sensation? Move the palms away again after only one to two seconds.

c. Next, hold you palms several inches away from the sides of the head. Again, slowly approach the palm until they are about 2 inches distant from the head. Can you notice the aura? Move the palms away again.

d. Checking near the shoulders

25   f. Smoothing the energy

d. Now, hold the palms several inches distant from the back of the shoulders. Approach them to about 2 inches away, and notice any sensations; then move the palms away again.

e. In this same way, proceed to other areas of the body, noticing the aura in each case—both front and back regions of the arms, lungs, heart, stomach area, lower back, hands, legs and feet—all major regions of the body. This takes about two to three minutes. At all times, we move our hands in a gentle manner, trying to disturb the person as little as possible. We breathe peacefully and naturally.

f. Finally, holding the palms a few inches away from the receiver, begin at the top of the head and make long, gentle motions along the entire length of the person, as though smoothing their energy that you may have disturbed, taking about fifteen to thirty seconds.

While doing this exercise, it is remarkable to think that we are touching a part of the living person, although it is an invisible part. Often the receiver will notice sensations during this exercise, and it is interesting for the giver and receiver to spend a few minutes comparing notes afterward.

Aura Interpretation.   In doing the foregoing exercise, we notice that the aura changes quality from one place to another. The front may be different from the back, the upper part may be different from the lower part, and there may be small areas near certain organs that are different from others. These differences may be noticed through variations in sensation such as the following:
- Warm spots and cool spots
- Smooth spots and rough spots
- Areas that feel flat or sunken, and areas that feel rounded or puffy
- Heavy, dense spots and light, insubstantial spots

Other sensations may also be noticed. In fact, each person seems to sense these different qualities in a slightly different way, almost as though we each had our language of aura interpretation. These various sensations indicate different conditions in the energy flow, and in the physical body. An overly warm spot, for example, may show an area of excessive discharge. An overly cool spot may show that energy flow is blocked or impeded in that place. A rough spot may indicate an area of discharge or irritation. A spot that seems to pull our hand in, may be seeking energy. And a spot that radiates out, may have a healthy energy flow.

Through practice, we learn to "read" these signs for ourselves. But whatever sensations you notice, remember that in checking the aura, you are actually touching a part of the person, and maintain an attitude of care and respect.

26   1a. Beginning posture

C.   Clearing the Aura.   The practice of palm healing is intended to improve the condition of the aura or energy body. Our first step toward this goal is to break up and dissipate any stagnation that remains in the aura. In the section on *Preparation for the Giver*, we described clearing exercises that can be done by one person alone. Following, we offer examples of exercises in which the giver assists the receiver in clearing the aura. The receiver will benefit much more from palm healing if this type of clearing exercise has been practiced first.

27   1b. Extend the hands.

1. Clearing the Aura: Basic Exercise
  a.   The receiver sits in the Seiza or other sitting position, and holds the palms together in front of the chest in the Unifying Position. Eyes may be closed or open, breathing is natural and peaceful. The giver takes the same posture

28 1b. Spread the hands.

29 1b. Clap.

and sits and the receiver's back, about 2 to 3 feet distant.

30 2a. Beginning posture

b. The giver extends the hands, spreads them wide, then claps sharply two times with a slight pause between claps. The sharp, clear sound vibrations help to break up and disperse stagnant energy.

Repeat clapping again if desired.

c. Giver and receiver breathe in deeply and chant the sound "Su" together several times, regulating and harmonizing energy flow.

d. Lower the hands and relax.

2. Clearing the Aura: Comprehensive Exercise

a. The giver and receiver take the same posture as in the first exercise, sitting with hands in the Unifying Position, the giver at the receiver's back. If the receiver is sitting in a chair, the giver may stand.

32 2b. Clap right.

31 2b. Clap.

66

33 2b. Clap left.

34 2c. Brush down.

35 2d. Brush up.

36 2e. Blow.

Step *c*: Brushing down
at the sides of the head

Step *d*: Brushing
up at the sides of
the head

b. The giver extends the hands and claps sharply two times at the back of the receiver's neck, then, two times at the left side of the head near the ear, then, two times at the back again, then, two times at the right side of the head, and finally two claps at the back.

c. The giver brushes downward three times at the sides of the receiver's head, very briskly, as if creating a wind to blow away stagnation.

d. Then, the giver brushes upward three times, very briskly.

e. The giver moves close to the back of the receiver's neck and blows a sudden, sharp, cold breath into the back of the neck. The mouth forms the sound "whoooo" about 2 inches distant, but the breath is blown silently. This helps to disperse stagnant energy.

Step *e*: Blowing breath into
the back of the neck

f. Both giver and receiver sit quietly and relax for a moment.

3. Clearing the Aura: Additional Suggestions.   While practicing palm healing, stagnant energy may be further discharged, and it is sometimes helpful to practice a brief aura-clearing exercise before continuing. One or more of the following steps can be used. This may be done at the end of an exercise, or even in the middle if desired.

a. *Clapping.*   Use sharp, clear claps to quickly disperse stagnation, in one of the following patterns:
  • Two sharp claps at the back.
  • Two claps each at the back, left, back, right, back, this series repeated one or more times.
  • Spread the hands wide apart and clap once, loud and sharply. Pause for a moment and clap again and slowly increase the speed of clapping until you are clapping very fast and softly, creating a fine vibration.

b. *Chanting.*   Chant several times to disperse stagnation and unify vibrations. The sound "Su" has an even, harmonious effect. "A-U-M" is unifying and powerful. "Toh" clears and disperses stagnation.

c. *Blowing.*   Use your breath to create a sharp, strong, cold stream of air with a focused feeling. This can help disperse stagnation at the back of the neck or at the hair spiral on top of the head.

d. *Brushing.*   Holding your hands several inches from the body, make brisk brushing motions as if to clear the air, as shown in the Comprehensive Exercise for aura clearing.

e. *Regenerating.*   Any of the steps used to Generate Healing Ability can be helpful when dispersing stagnation, to confirm a positive flow of healing force.

Harmonizng the Whole Body's Energy Flow

The preparatory steps of calming the mind, clearing the aura and generating healing ability pave the way for balancing and reinforcing the energy of the body as a whole. There are many exercises that can be used for a general, overall unifying and harmonizing of our energy. They leave us with a feeling of energy, completeness, and well-being. Because of their beneficial effect upon our body and energy system as a whole, one, two, three, or more of this type of exercise may be used in a single practice session. Following are several examples.

1. Energizing the Spiritual Channel.   By strengthening the energy flow through the spiritual channel, we energize and harmonize the whole body.

a. Giver and receiver both sit in the Seiza or other sitting posture, hands held in front of the chest in the Unifying Position. The giver sits behind the receiver's back, just over an arm's length away. Both giver and receiver breathe with natural, peaceful breathing.

37 1c. Extend hands toward the shoulders.

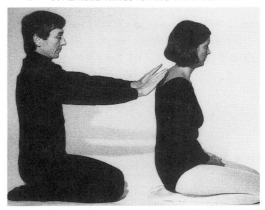

b. The giver claps two times to clear residual stagnation.

c. The giver extends the palm toward the receiver's back, not touching the back but about 1 to 2 inches away, palms aimed at the back at a 45-degree angle.

38 1d. Move hands to the base of the spine, and up again.

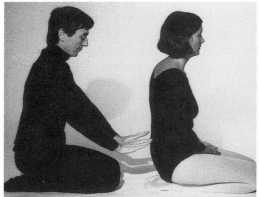

39 1e. Finish at center back.

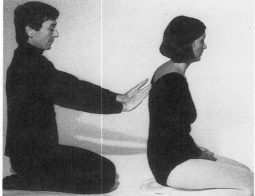

40 2b. Clap.

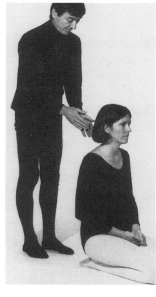

d. Beginning at the top of the spine, at the base of the neck, the giver slowly moves the hands down the length of the spine and back up again, while both giver and receiver chant "Su." Repeat five times.

e. Finally, the giver holds the palms at the center of the back at the heart area and chants "Su" three times. Hold the hands quietly in that position for a moment, then withdraw the hands and relax.

2. Harmonizing the Head Spiral. This exercise may be used for both clearing and harmonizing, since it has elements of both. The harmonizing element is the care given to the head spiral, reinforcing, pacifying and strengthening the direction of our natural energy flow.

a. The receiver sits with hands in the Unifying

41 2c. Make a spiral.   **42** 2d. Brush up.   **43** 2d. Brush down.

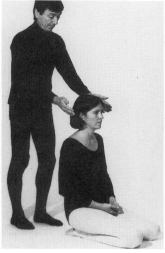

Step *c*: Clockwise spiral over woman's head, counterclockwise over man's

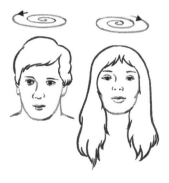

Position. The giver sits up on the knees to gain height, or may stand, hands also in the Unifying Position. Both giver and receiver breathe naturally and peacefully. The receiver's eyes may be closed or gently open.

b. The giver extends the hands and claps two times, first at the back of the receiver's neck, then to the left, again at the back, then to the right, and finally again at the back.

c. The giver holds one palm 1 to 2 inches above the top of the receiver's head, and begins to make a peaceful, spirallic motion. If the receiver is a man, the spiral should be counterclockwise; if a woman, clockwise, following the natural tendency of Heaven's or Earth's force in each one. The spirallic motion should be peaceful, orderly, and even (if not, it may create a disturbed feeling for the receiver—as would a spiral going the wrong direction). Continue silently, or if desired, both may chant "Su," two to three minutes, or until the receiver feels peaceful and balanced.

d. The giver brushes the hands briskly upward around the head three times, then briskly downward three times, as described in the exercises for clearing the aura.

e. The giver blows a strong, focused, cold breath at the back of the receiver's neck, very sharply, to disperse stagnation.

f. Repeat step *b* above, clapping as described to further clear stagnation away.

g. Relax and sit quietly for a moment.

70

44 2e. Blow.

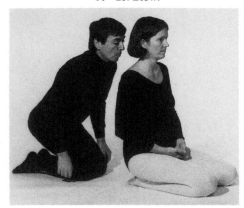

45 3b. Holding the hand points

3. Balancing Inner-Outer, Left-Right Energy. The center of the palm is a major energy center of the body, and relates to the inner organs to activate and harmonize energy flow. In this exercise we use the center points of both palms of the receiver to unify the energies of the right and left sides together with this inside-outside polarity, thus increasing and harmonizing the whole body's energy flow.

    a.   The receiver may sit on the floor or in a chair; the giver may sit up on the knees or stand at the back. Both begin by taking the Unifying Position of the hands held palms together near the chest. Breathing is full and natural and eyes may be closed or gently open.

    b.   The receiver raises the hands to about shoulder level, and the giver gently holds the hands, placing the thumb spirals on the center points of the receiver's palm. Giver and receiver breathe in synchronization, and may chant "Su" together five to seven times, or until the receiver feels unified and energized.

    c.   Return hands to the Unifying Position, then relax.

Additional Exercises to Harmonize the Whole Body's Energy. There are many exercises that have a comprehensive effect, serving to unify and harmonize the whole body's energy. A number of these can be found in Chapters 5 through 11 of this book, such as the following:

    • Harmonizing the Triple Heater (Chapter 5)
    • Harmonizing the Five Colliding Places (Chapter 5)
    • Harmonizing the Nervous and Digestive Systems (Chapter 6)

This type of exercise is very beneficial and can make up an entire palm healing practice session without needing any specialized techniques in addition.

Exercises for Special Purposes

If the beginning steps of meditating, clearing, energizing, and balancing whole-body energy have been practiced well, it often happens that no specialized exercises are needed. Sometimes, however, the person receiving palm healing care may have special needs that are not met by these first, general steps. If so, exercises for special purposes can be introduced. Chapters 5 through 11 of this book describe many such exercises for specific purposes, using a variety of techniques, which may be used in this step, before moving on to the finishing steps of a palm healing session.

Exercises may be specifically geared to help a certain organ, chakra, area, or system of the body, as well as mental and emotional issues. We can utilize our understanding of the chakras, organs, meridians, points, sound, hand movements, and other factors to create such exercises. With practice and experience, we can learn to use a wide variety of specialized exercises for various circumstances.

Usually we do not recommend using more than a few specialized exercises at one time, to avoid overstimulation or confusion. It is better to keep it simple, and use just a few selected exercises focusing on one or two specific areas in a single session of palm healing. These should be followed by proper finalization steps to round out the session, leaving the receiver feeling peaceful and balanced.

Finalization

After receiving palm healing, we should feel peaceful, refreshed, energized, and balanced. If giving palm healing, we should have an increased sense of well-being too. To make sure that the session closes on a balanced note, proper finalization steps are important. If the palm healing session has been short and has included mainly general harmonizing exercises, only a brief period of finalization may be needed. If the session has been longer or included more specialized exercises, more time may be needed for finalization with the inclusion of extra harmonizing exercises. In both instances, the following pattern of finalization is recommended.

A. Checking the Aura. In the beginning, we checked the aura to become familiar with the receiver's energy flow. At the end, we check the aura again to make sure that the energy flow has improved and is in a healthy, balanced condition.

1. Final Checking of the Aura.
   a. The receiver sits in a comfortable position, or if already lying down, may continue to rest comfortably. Eyes may be closed or gently open.
   b. The giver begins by sitting with hands in the Unifying Position, palms to-gether in front of the chest—taking a moment to meditate peacefully and calm the mind.
   c. The giver extends the palms and gently moves them to sense the receiver's

46 1c. Checking the upper body   **47** 1c. Checking the lower body

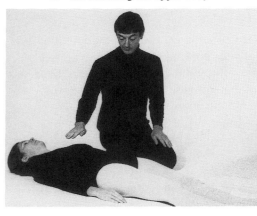 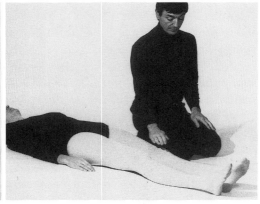

aura, taking two to three minutes. (Refer to the preparatory exercise on Checking the Aura for detailed instructions.) Notice all major areas of the aura and try to see if the energy flow feels balanced, or if not, become aware of what additional harmonizing steps may be needed. Move the palms in a gentle, continuous manner as though smoothing out the energy of the receiver. Move in either an upward or a downward direction, whichever feels better to the receiver.

d.   The giver may ask the receiver whether or not he or she feels comfortable and balanced. This also helps to determine what kind of final balancing exercises are needed.

e.   The giver returns to the peaceful sitting position.

B.   Clearing the Aura.   In this exercise, we help to release and disperse any remaining stagnated energy, including excess energy which may have been stirred up during palm healing exercises. We can use the Basic Exercise for clearing the aura described in the preparatory steps (page 64). The receiver may be sitting, or comfortably lying down. If desired, the more comprehensive aura-clearing exercise (page 65) may be used. In either case, after this step, both giver and receiver should feel more light, refreshed, and peaceful.

C.   Stabilization.   This step includes a final harmonization of energy flow for the whole body, leaving the receiver in a unified, peaceful state. Several exercises may be used for this purpose. Some recommended examples follow.

1.   Additional Harmonizing Exercises.   If it is needed or desired, extra harmonizing exercises may be added in this step. Examples from section on Harmonizing the Whole Body's Energy Flow may be used, such as those using the head spiral and the spiritual channel. One or more harmonizing exercises may be chosen depending on whether the receiver feels generally peaceful or balanced, or not. Both giver and receiver should have a sense of well-being before ending the palm healing practice.

2. Hara-Forehead Stabilization. Whole-body energy flow is unified and strengthened in a very peaceful, stabilizing manner by forming a circuit between two complementary energy centers that affect our vitality and well-being.

a. The receiver may sit or lie down comfortably and relax, eyes closed, breathing peacefully. The giver sits at the side and begins by calming the mind for a moment, hands in the Unifying Position in front of the chest.

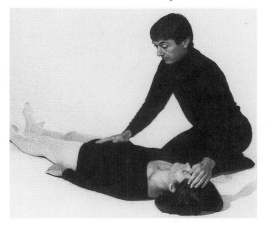

48 2b. Hara-forehead position

b. The giver extends the palms, placing one over the hara region (two finger-widths below the navel), the other over the forehead. The palms may touch the receiver or may be held just slightly above the surface of the body, about 1 inch away, as desired.

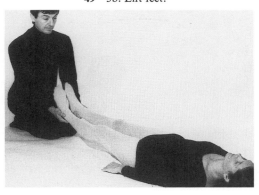

49 3b. Lift feet.

c. The giver's breathing can follow that of the receiver, so that both are breathing at the same time, peacefully. The giver may chant "Su" on the exhalation if desired. Continue two to three minutes, allowing energy to flow through the hands and energy centers, forming a secure circuit. You may keep a mental image of peace and harmony.

d. Gently remove the hands and relax.

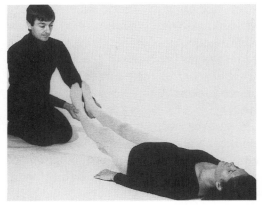

50 3b. Sway feet to one side.

3. Foot Stabilization. Touching the feet creates a downward, stabilizing energy flow and is particularly helpful for people who seem to have too much energy in the upper part of the body, or who need to come "down to earth."

a. The receiver lies down comfortably on the back and relaxes, breathing peacefully.

b. The giver kneels at the feet and gently holds the feet, lifting them

1 to 2 inches off the floor and swaying the legs just a few inches side-to-side several times, then gently placing the feet back on the floor.

c. Next, the giver gently grasps the feet and places the thumb spirals over the central point on the soles of the feet. Hold this position two to three minutes, breathing

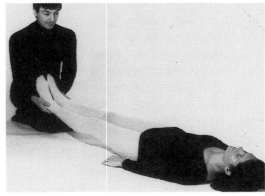

51 3b. Sway feet to the other side.

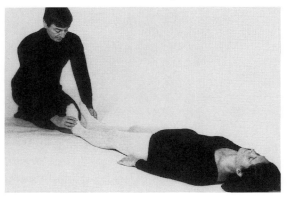

52 3c. Hold foot points.

peacefully, following the breath of the receiver. If desired, the giver may chant "Su." Keep a mental image of harmony, stability, and peace.

d. Gently remove the hands and relax.

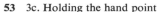

53 3c. Holding the hand point

4. Hand Stabilization. The central point in the palm of the hand influences the whole body's energy flow. This exercise utilizes that point to harmonize, unify, and stabilize the receiver's energy.

a. The receiver may sit or lie down comfortably and the giver sits to the side. Both breathe naturally and peacefully, eyes closed or slightly open.

b. The giver takes the receiver's hand, using either the center of the palm or the thumb spiral, to touch the receiver's central palm point. The giver follows the breathing speed of the receiver and may chant if desired, using the sound "Su" or "A-U-M." Continue two to three minutes. A mental image of peace, harmony, unity, and stability may also be kept.

c. Remove the hand and relax.

Rest

After finishing palm healing practice, allow a few minutes for rest. The receiver can rest sitting or lying down, and gradually begin to move around and get up after a while. It is better to do quiet activities for a while and leave noisy or vigorous activities until later. Then, the flow of energy is not disturbed and the receiver can feel energized and refreshed for some time.

The giver may also rest, or may prefer to rinse the hands and then do some kind of contrasting activity.

It is interesting for the giver and receiver to spend a few minutes talking and exchanging thoughts about the palm healing practice. Both can learn from hearing what the other noticed and experienced.

Following palm healing practice, both giver and receiver should feel happy, energized, balanced, and peaceful.

Study Suggestion

To learn palm healing, we need to experience both giving and receiving, and we need to learn specific exercises as well as experiencing the flow of the pattern as a whole. You may wish to spend time concentrating on learning each separate exercise, and then practice them as a pattern, choosing just one exercise in each category. In palm healing practice completing the entire pattern may take anywhere from ten minutes to one hour or more, depending on your needs. Practice the exercises with a friend or family member, and then change places and reverse roles.

Chapter 5

Using the Chakras for Healing

Chakras are major energy centers of the body, places where life energy is especially concentrated. They serve to gather energy, regulate it, and circulate it to the surrounding organs. *Chakra* is a Sanskrit word meaning "wheel," referring to the moving, spirallic form taken by the chakras.

Since the chakras are important centers of life energy, palm healing exercises using the chakras are very effective. Chakra exercises may be used for a general harmonizing of bodily energy, to strengthen the energy flow in a specific region of the body, to help a certain organ, and to improve mental and emotional functions.

Functions of the Major Chakras

Seven major chakras are generally recognized, as well as a number of minor chakras, as shown in the illustration.[1] In general, the upper chakras govern the more yin functions of thinking, seeing, and speaking, while the lower chakras govern the more yang functions of digestion, reproduction, and elimination. The upper, yinner chakras tend to be more expanded, while the lower, more yang chakras tend to be more contracted. Following is a description of the seven major chakras and the secondary hand and foot chakras—their location, organs and functions they govern, and qualities that they influence.

• *The First Chakra: The Base Chakra*
   Location: Base of the spine

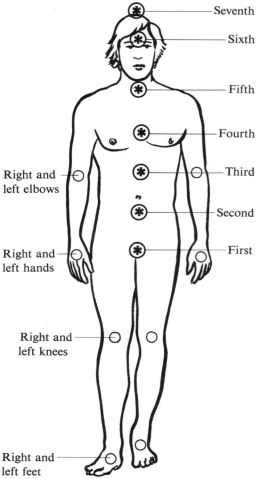

The Seven Major Chakras and Eight Secondary Chakras

Seventh
Sixth
Fifth
Fourth
Right and left elbows
Third
Second
First
Right and left hands
Right and left knees
Right and left feet

---

[1] Among various schools of thought, there are different opinions as to the exact number and location of the major chakras.

Organs and functions: Bladder and rectum, reproductive organs, and part of the nervous and circulatory functions

Qualities produced: Physical and mental harmony with the Earth and atmosphere; strengthens sexual vitality and our ability to adapt to our surroundings.

- *The Second Chakra: The Sacral Chakra or Hara*

    Location: Lower abdominal region, about two finger-widths below the navel

    Organs and functions: Intestinal digestion and absorption, secretion of digestive fluids; reproductive functions, including the ovaries, pregnancy, and hormones. The hara functions as the central administrator for the physical body.

    Qualities produced: Physical stability, mental confidence

- *The Third Chakra: The Solar Plexus Chakra*

    Location: Solar plexus-stomach region, about 2 inches below the base of the sternum

    Organs and functions: Stomach, spleen, pancreas, liver, gallbladder, kidneys; the secretion of hormones and digestive liquids in this area

    Qualities produced: Physical and mental powers, including unusual ability to control physical movement, and unusual powers which require good balance among all physical movements

- *The Fourth Chakra: The Heart Chakra*

    Location: Over the heart, at the center of the breastbone

    Organs and functions: Heart and circulation, charging the blood and body fluids with energy, including the lymph; also influences breathing and digestion. This chakra functions as the central administrator for the whole body's energy flow.

    Qualities produced: Emotional feeling, including love and sympathy toward others; sensitive perception in relation to the environment

- *The Fifth Chakra: The Throat Chakra*

    Location: Center of the throat, between the jaw and the base of the throat

    Organs and functions: Respiration and vocalization, and the motion of the tongue, as well as saliva production and functions of the bronchi

    Qualities produced: Intellectual and logical expression, and artistic expression

- *The Sixth Chakra: The Ajna Chakra or Third Eye*

    Location: Slightly above and between the eyebrows

    Organs and functions: The midbrain; nerve stimulations are assimilated here and distributed to all parts of the brain. The midbrain acts as the central administrator for the head region.

    Qualities produced: Control of consciousness and physical reactions, purification of thoughts into more concentrated forms of thinking, with the gradual diminishing of sensory perception

- *The Seventh Chakra: The Crown Chakra*

  Location: Top of the head and extending above the head several inches

  Organs and functions: The brain cortex and various kinds of consciousness, including the unification of spiritual, mental, and physical activities

  Qualities produced: Consciousness expansion toward the development of universal understanding, diminishing egocentric thinking

- *Secondary Hand Chakras*

  Location: The central points of the palms, the acupuncture point called *Rō-Kyū*, Heart Governor #8, the "Heart of the Hand"

  Organs and functions: The hand chakras function as extensions of the fourth, heart chakra. The right-hand chakra governs discharge of energy toward the periphery, which has been produced by the other chakras. The left-hand chakra governs the active reception of energy from the surrounding atmosphere, which feeds the various chakras.

- *Secondary Foot Chakras*

  Location: The central points of the soles of the feet, called *Soku-Shin* in acupuncture, the "Heart of the Foot"

  Organs and functions: The two foot chakras act as extensions of the Second, sacral chakra or hara. The left-foot chakra governs the discharge of energy toward the Earth from various body chakras, and the right-foot chakra governs reception of energy from the Earth, nourishing various body chakras.

Additional Chakras. The knees, elbows, and other points are often referred to as secondary chakras as well.

Palm Healing Exercises Using the Chakras

As with all palm healing exercises, applications involving the chakras are meant to be used in the context of the whole palm healing pattern described in Chapter 4.

1. Locating the Chakras. Through this exercise we become familiar with the location of each chakra and notice the type of energy each one has. This exercise is designed for two people, but it is also possible to locate your own chakras. Each chakra feels a little different from the others, and they also vary from person to person.

1 1a, b. Beginning posture

    a. The receiver sits or lies down comfortably, eyes closed or partly open, breathing naturally. The giver sits to the side, or may stand if the receiver is sitting in a chair.

2

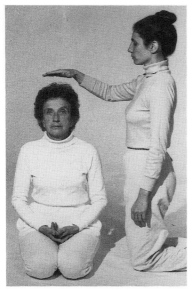

1c. Checking the seventh Chakra

b. The giver may begin by sitting peacefully for a moment, hands in the Unifying Position, to calm the mind.

c. The giver extends one palm to the top of the receiver's head, pausing about 1 inch above the head. Move the palm slowly, gently back and forth, noticing the dense, magnetic feeling as the hand passes through the seventh chakra. Spend about fifteen seconds.

d. Next, the giver raises the palm about 10 inches above the receiver's head, then lowers the palm to about 1 inch away, again noticing the increasingly dense, magnetic sensation of the chakra as the hand approaches. Continue slowly, gently bouncing the hand in this way for about fifteen seconds, noticing the chakra.

e. Now, repeat this same procedure (steps c and

3 1c. Checking side-to-side   **4** 1d. Checking up-and-down   **5** 1e. Sixth Chakra

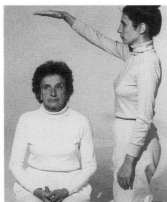

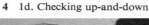

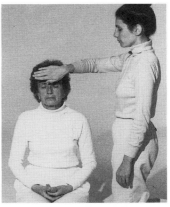

6 1e. Fifth Chakra   **7** 1e. Fourth Chakra   **8** 1e. Third Chakra

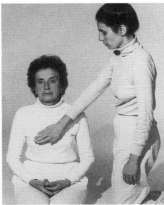

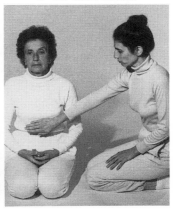

9 1e. Second Chakra

10 1e. First Chakra, on back

11 1e. First Chakra, on front

12 1g. Elbows

13 1g. Knees

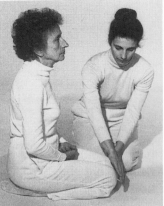

14 1g. Soles of the feet

15 1g. Palms of the hands

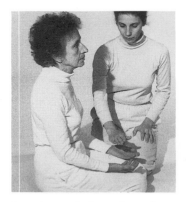

d) at the sixth chakra between and slightly above the eyebrows, holding the palm in front, and at the fifth, throat chakra, the fourth, heart chakra, the third, solar plexus chakra, and the second, hara chakra. Notice how each one differs or is unique. At the same time, the receiver can notice any effects from this brief, gentle checking exercise.

f. The first, root chakra may be checked on the back, holding the palm at the base of the spine, or on the front, holding the palm one-third of the way down the thighs, facing the torso.

g. Next, check the central points of the palms of the hands, and the soles of the feet. You may also check the knees and elbows if desired.

h. Finish by smoothing down the receiver's energy field with three to five long, smooth, head-to-toe movements of the palms, a few inches away from the surface of the body.

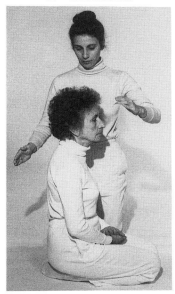

16   1h. Smoothe.

Characteristics that you may notice about each chakra include its size, shape, density, temperature, strength, and texture. These characteristics may change from time to time depending on the influences affecting the chakras as well as the whole aura.

2.   Simple Chakra Care.   If you wish to energize, strengthen, or unify a certain chakra's energy flow, this exercise is helpful. You may wish to help a particular chakra because one of the nearby organs that it governs is weak, or because of the mental and emotional benefits associated with that chakra, or because in checking the chakra, you have noticed a lack of energy. This exercise is designed for two persons, but may also be done alone and is very good personal care.

    a.   The receiver sits comfortably or may lie down, breathing peacefully, eyes closed or partly open. The giver sits at the side, and may begin with the hands in the Unifying Position for a moment to calm the mind and unify energy.

    b.   The giver extends one palm to the chakra that has been selected, and either places the palm gently on the spot, or holds the palm 1/2 to 1 inch above, not touching, as preferred. The giver breathes in harmony with the receiver, following the same speed of breathing. The giver may choose to chant on the exhalation, using the sound "Su." Continue two to three minutes, keeping a mental image of peace and harmony.

    c.   Gently remove the hand when the chakra feels refreshed and strengthened.

    d.   Also try this exercise with one palm on the front and the other palm on the back of the chakra. This has a stronger effect.

    e.   Try several chakras and see how you can improve their condition, as well as the resulting benefits to your physical and mental condition.

    f.   Sit with hands in the Unifying Position again, then relax.

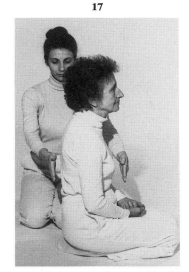

17

2d. Chakra care, front and back

3.   Triple Heater Harmonization.   The Second, Third, and Fourth Chakras (Hara, Solar Plexus, and Heart respectively) make up the central points of the Triple Heater, as it is called in Oriental medicine. These three chakras have the important function of regulating some of our most vital internal organs, controlling metabo-

18 3c. Lower Heater

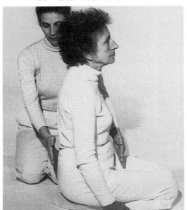

19 3f. Upper Heater

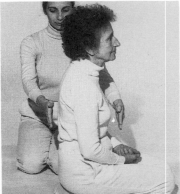

20 3g. Clap in front.

21 3g. Clap in back.

lism or heat production. In this exercise, we give palm healing care to these Triple Heater areas in order to strengthen and unify central-body functions, and harmonize internal heat.

a. The receiver sits in the Seiza or other position, breathing naturally, eyes closed or partly open. Hands may be in the Unifying Position or folded in the lap.

b. The giver sits to the side, taking the same position, and begins with hands in the Unifying Position.

c. Beginning with the second chakra (hara), the giver places one palm over the front and one palm over the back at the same area. The palms may touch receiver or may be held about 1 inch away if desired.

d. Both giver and receiver breathe together with natural, full, peaceful breaths, and may chant "Su" if desired. Continue two to three minutes, or chant about ten times.

e. Next, the giver moves the palm up to the third chakra (solar plexus) and repeats steps *c* and *d*.

f. The giver then moves the palms up to the fourth chakra (heart) and repeats steps *c* and *d*.

g. The giver claps two times, briefly, front and back, to help release stagnated energy.

h. Lower the hands, sit quietly for a moment, and relax.

Upward versus Downward Direction. In the foregoing exercise, we began with the lower chakra, and worked our way upward to the higher chakras. This is working in a yin, upward direction and produces an effect of more lightness, coolness, and mental activity. If we wish, we can alternatively practice the same exercise (or any other exercise) in a downward direction, to produce more yang effects of warmth, stabilization, and physical activity.

4. Harmonizing the Five Colliding Places.

Oriental medicine practitioners sometimes called the chakras "colliding places" since they act as crossroads for the pathways of energy running through our body. In this exercise, we give palm healing care to the five central chakras to harmonize the energy of the entire body.

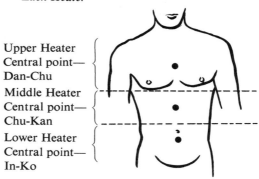

The Triple Heater with Central Points for Each Heater

Upper Heater
Central point—
Dan-Chu

Middle Heater
Central point—
Chu-Kan

Lower Heater
Central point—
In-Ko

a. The receiver sits comfortably, breathing naturally, eyes closed or gently open, hands in the lap or in the Unifying Position. The giver sits at the side in the same posture, hands in the Unifying Position.

b. The giver extends the palms, and begins with the second chakra (hara), one palm at the front, the other at the back, either touching or not touching (1 inch away) as preferred.

22 4a. Starting posture

c. The giver follows the breathing speed of the receiver and both breathe together naturally and harmoniously. Chanting "Su" may be added if desired. Continue two to three minutes, allowing energy to flow.

d. The giver gently removes the palms and moves them up to the third chakra (solar plexus), repeating steps *b* and *c*.

Harmonizing the Five Colliding Places: positions for hands in steps *b-h*, beginning with the second chakra and working upward

e. Next, the giver proceeds to the fourth chakra (heart) and repeats the same process.

f. The giver moves the palms up to the fifth chakra (throat) and repeats steps *b* and *c* again.

g. The giver again repeats this process at the sixth chakra (midbrain or *ajna* chakra).

h. To finish, the giver gently lifts the palms in an upward

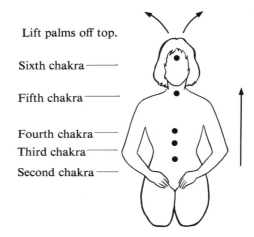

Lift palms off top.

Sixth chakra

Fifth chakra

Fourth chakra
Third chakra
Second chakra

84

direction (see illustration). Then, relax.

Note on Upward Versus Downward Direction. Exercise 4 has been directed in a yin, upward direction, resulting in a greater feeling of lightness, coolness, and gentleness. This direction may also be reversed as we see in the next exercise.

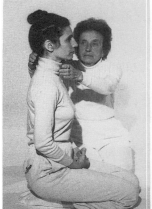

5. Harmonizing the Five Colliding Places: Variation. This exercise is similar to Exercise 4, but it is done in a downward direction and finished with a more yang final step to achieve overall harmonization.

Harmonizing the Five Colliding Places: Variation. Step *b* utilizes the five central chakras beginning with sixth and moving downward. Dots show position of hands in step *c*.

Step *c*

Sixth chakra

Fifth chakra

Fourth chakra

Third chakra

Second chakra

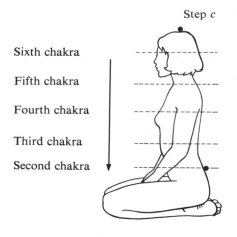

a. The giver and receiver position themselves as in Exercise 4.

b. The giver gives palm healing care to each of the five central chakras as described in Exercise 4, this time beginning with the sixth chakra (midbrain or *ajna*) and working downward, finishing with the second chakra (hara).

c. Next, the giver places one palm at the back position of the second chakra, and the other palm at the top of the head. This represents the lower and upper ends of the spiritual channel. Both giver and receiver breathe naturally and fully, allowing energy to flow and chanting "Su" or "A-U-M" if desired. This helps to unify the energy of the spiritual channel and consequently of the whole body.

d. Remove the hands and relax.

6. Chakra Care on the Back. In this exercise we make use of the relationship between the lower and upper chakras to bring energy to the whole length of the nervous system along the back. The whole body's energy flow is affected and harmonized, and especially the back.

a. The receiver sits in the Seiza or other comfortable posture, eyes closed or half open, hands in the lap or in the Unifying Position. The receiver sits to the side near the back, hands in the Unifying Position. Both giver and receiver breathe together peacefully and may chant if desired.

b. The giver places one hand at the base of the spine, on the back position

25

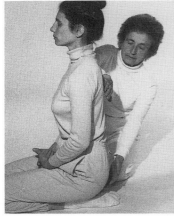

6c. First and Fourth Chakras

26

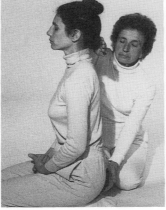

6d. First and Fifth Chakras

27

6e. First and Seventh Chakras

28

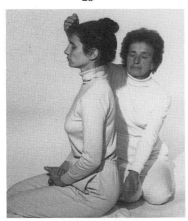

6f. First Chakra and Forehead

of the first chakra (base or root chakra), and the other palm on the back position of the third chakra (solar plexus). Continue in this position two to three minutes, maintaining peaceful breathing, allowing energy to flow.

c. Keeping one palm at the first chakra, the giver moves the other palm up to the back of the fourth, heart chakra, and proceeds as above.

d. Keeping the same palm at the first chakra, the giver moves the other palm further up, to the back of the fifth, throat chakra, and repeats the same procedure.

e. Continuing with the palm at the first chakra, the giver moves the other palm on up to the seventh, crown chakra at the top of the head, and proceeds as above.

f. Finally, with the first palm still at the base of the spine, the giver places the other palm gently on the receiver's forehead. Now, the palms are touching both the beginning point and the end point of the back nervous system. Again continue two to three minutes to breathe peacefully, allowing energy to flow, and chanting if desired.

g. Remove the palms and relax.

Chakra Care on the Back: Steps *b-f*. One hand remains on the back of the first chakra, while the other hand moves to the positions shown.

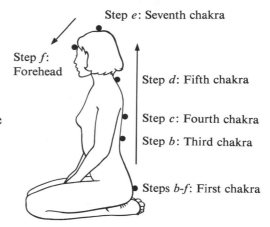

Step *e*: Seventh chakra

Step *f*: Forehead

Step *d*: Fifth chakra

Step *c*: Fourth chakra

Step *b*: Third chakra

Steps *b-f*: First chakra

Quick Variation—Back Exercise. If there is very little time, you may do a short version of this exercise simply by placing one palm at the base of the spine, the other palm on the forehead, and holding two to three minutes while breathing naturally and perhaps chanting. This covers the beginning and end points of the back nervous system. However, it is much more effective if the comprehensive exercise can be done.

7. Chakra Care on the Front. Utilizing the front chakra positions, we can especially strengthen the digestive system and other vital organs. This is done in the same manner as the preceding exercise on the back. As always, the giver may either touch the receiver, or not touch, holding the palms 1/2 to 1 inch away, as preferred.

    a.   The giver and receiver take the same posture as in Exercise 6, this time the giver is positioned closer to the front.

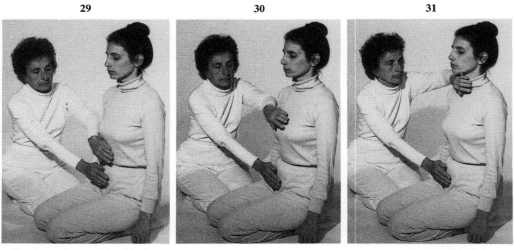

   29   30   31

7b. Second and Third Chakras   7c. Second and Fourth Chakras   7d. Second and Fifth Chakras

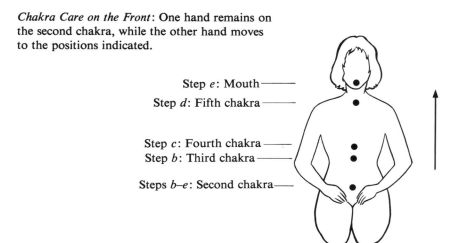

Chakra Care on the Front: One hand remains on the second chakra, while the other hand moves to the positions indicated.

Step *e*: Mouth

Step *d*: Fifth chakra

Step *c*: Fourth chakra

Step *b*: Third chakra

Steps *b–e*: Second chakra

b. The giver places one palm at the second chakra (hara) of the receiver and the other palm at the solar plexus (third chakra). Hold two to three minutes, breathing naturally, chanting if desired, and allowing energy to flow.

c. Keeping one palm at the second chakra, the giver moves the other up to the fourth chakra (heart) and proceeds as above.

d. With the first palm remaining at the second chakra, the giver moves the other up to the fifth chakra (throat) and repeats this process.

e. Finally, with the first palm still at the second chakra, the giver places the other palm gently at the mouth of the receiver. Now, the palms are covering the beginning and lower portion of the digestive system. Proceed as above.

f. Gently remove the hands and relax.

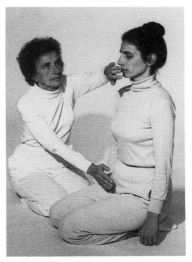

32

7e. Second Chakra and Mouth

8. Harmonizing Head and Throat Chakras. The flow of energy through the head region is harmonized and strengthened in this exercise, using the fifth chakra at the throat, and the seventh chakra on top of the head. This practice is helpful for calming the thoughts, harmonizing the nervous system, energizing the will and spirituality, and promoting confidence and ability in expression. The head is a compact version of the whole body, and any care given to the head region also reflects in the rest of the body as well.

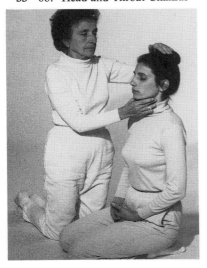

33 8b. Head and Throat Chakras

a. The receiver sits in a comfortable position, eyes closed or slightly open, hands in the lap or in the Unifying Position held near the throat, for best effect.

b. The giver sits or stands to the side, and places one palm on the top of the receiver's head, and the other palm gently over the region of the throat. (As you can see in the picture, this is also near the root of the tongue.)

c. Breathing together fully and naturally, the giver chants "Su," to increase and harmonize energy, while the receiver chants "Mmmm," to focus energy in his own head region. If possible, the receiver curls the tongue upward inside the mouth so that the tip of the tongue touches the palate (roof of the mouth). This creates a stronger connection

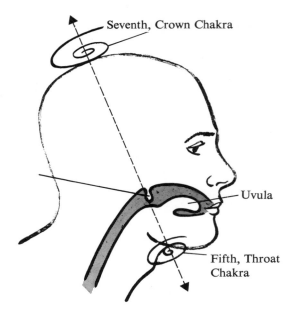

for the energy flowing up and down through the head. Continue two to three minutes, or chant about ten times.

    d.   Remove the hands and relax.

Additional Suggestions

The exercises presented in this chapter can serve as basic examples to use in palm healing practice for the chakras. Other exercises involving the chakras can also be created, using good technique with preparation and finalizing steps. Up-down relationships among the chakras may be used, as well as front-back variations, and various interrelationships among the organs and regions of the body in relation to the chakras.

Chapter 6
Palm Healing for the Internal Organs

Our internal organs, which sustain our vital functions, are in turn sustained by the flow of life energy that nourishes and activates them. Through palm healing, we can strengthen this energy flow and improve the functioning of our organs. Interrelationships among the organs are harmonized, imbalances are adjusted, and our system functions more smoothly as a result.

In order to practice palm healing for the internal organs, we first need to know the location and function of each one. A good book on anatomy and physiology is helpful, as are classes by qualified teachers, in both the modern, Western approach and the ancient, Oriental approach. Here, we include an illustration showing the positions of the major organs in general, as a starting point.

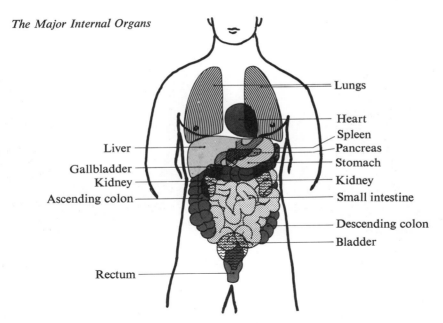

The Major Internal Organs

Lungs

Heart
Spleen
Pancreas
Stomach
Kidney
Small intestine

Liver
Gallbladder
Kidney
Ascending colon

Descending colon
Bladder

Rectum

1. Locating the Major Organs.   In this exercise, we use our palms to sense the energy of each major organ, one by one. By noticing the type of energy over and around an organ, we can tell a lot about its condition. Is it yang or yin, warm or cool, irritated or comfortable, full of energy or lacking in energy? These conditions may change from one day to the next depending on many influences, as we have already discussed, such as diet, lifestyle, weather, and activity.

This exercise is designed for two people, but we may also practice locating our own organs. Before beginning, please practice the steps for calming the mind, clearing the aura, and generating healing ability.

1 1a. Starting posture

a. The receiver sits comfortably or lies down, eyes closed or partly open, breathing naturally. The giver sits to the side and begins with hands in the Unifying Position.

b. The giver extends one palm, keeping the other hand in the lap. Move the palm to the selected organ, pausing about 1/2 to 1 inch above the surface of the body.

c. Move the hand gently and slowly side-to-side over the organ, noticing any sensations such as magnetic density, electricity, warmth, and so on.

d. Now raise the palm 6 to 10 inches above the organ, and slowly approach again to about 1/2 to 1 inch. Gently bounce the hand in this way several times, noticing the energy as the hand gets closer.

2 1b. Checking the organ   **3 1d. Ten inches over the organ**   **4 1f. Smoothe.**

e. Remove the hand and move on to another organ, repeating the same process (steps *b* through *d*). Try several major organs in this same manner—liver, heart, large intestine, small intestine, stomach, spleen-pancreas, right lung, left lung, kidneys, and others. Take one to two minutes for each.

f. When finished, smooth down the whole body's energy with several long, smooth, head-to-toe movements of the palms.

g. Sit peacefully again and relax.

When practicing this exercise for the first time, you may not notice very clear, precise perceptions. Do not worry. This comes with practice. Simply concentrate on locating each organ's position, see if any perceptions are noticed, and enjoy learning this process.

2. Simple Palm Healing Care for One Organ. In this exercise, we aim to improve the quality and quantity of energy flowing through an organ.

a. The receiver may sit comfortably or lie down, eyes closed or partly open, breathing naturally. The giver sits at the side, with natural breathing, and begins with hands in the Unifying Position.

b. Selecting one organ, the giver extends one palm, keeping the other hand in the lap, and briefly checks the energy of the organ as described in Exercise 1.

c. Next, the giver gently rests the palm over the organ (or may hold the palm 1/2 to 1 inch above if desired). The other hand may be in the lap, or held up to draw in Heaven's force, or held down to draw up Earth's force. The giver follows the breathing of the receiver and the two breathe together in a natural, peaceful fashion. Chanting may be added if desired. Mental imagery may be used, visualizing a flow of healing energy through the organ. Continue two to five minutes and notice any perceptions experienced by the giver and the receiver.

5 2c. Palm healing for one organ

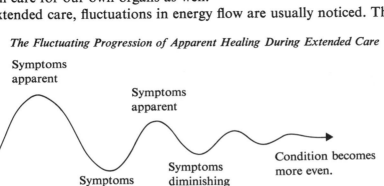

d. Recheck the energy of the organ as in step *b*. Is it the same as before, or has it changed?

e. Try other organs in the same way if desired.

f. Spend a moment to smooth the body's energy, especially if more than one organ has been worked on.

g. Remove the hands and relax; giver and receiver may discuss their experiences.

3. Extend Care for One Organ. When we wish to give extra care to a specific organ, we may practice palm healing for a longer time: ten minutes, twenty minutes, even one hour or more. The following exercise is for two persons, but we can practice such care for our own organs as well.

During extended care, fluctuations in energy flow are usually noticed. The heal-

The Fluctuating Progression of Apparent Healing During Extended Care

Symptoms
apparent

Symptoms
apparent

Symptoms
diminishing

Symptoms
diminishing

Condition becomes
more even.

ing process does not follow a straight line, so to speak, but can better be described as a fluctuating wave, as shown in the accompanying illustration.

In the beginning, the receiver notices an improvement in the condition for several minutes. This is followed by a period of several minutes when the symptoms reappear and this is followed again by apparent improvement. These ups and downs continue but with decreasing extremes, eventually evening out into a general, progressive betterment.

At the same time, the giver may notice similar fluctuations in the perceptions in the palms—first an increase in energy, then a decrease, then again an increase. At times, the giver may feel that his or her hands are absorbing stagnated energy. This may occur when a discharge of stagnated energy is occurring from the receiver. Some people giving palm healing care even feel discomfort or pain, as though taking on the adverse symptoms of the receiver. This can be stopped if the giver temporarily removes the hands and rests for a few minutes. He or she may also refresh the palms using various methods described in Chapter 4, before resuming.

The receiver can usually relax quietly during palm healing care, but should tell the giver if any discomfort occurs. The giver can remove his or her hands at that time and allow the receiver to rest, or else change the manner of palm healing, perhaps giving a general harmonizing exercise, and then deciding whether to return to the original exercise.

The overall direction of the palm healing session should be toward increasing improvement. Both the giver and receiver should feel good. The giver will feel refreshed rather than tired if the session has been managed well.

    a.   The receiver sits or lies down in a relaxed, comfortable posture. Hands are relaxed, eyes closed or partly open. Breathing is natural and peaceful.

    b.   The giver sits at the side, also in a comfortable, straight sitting posture, with

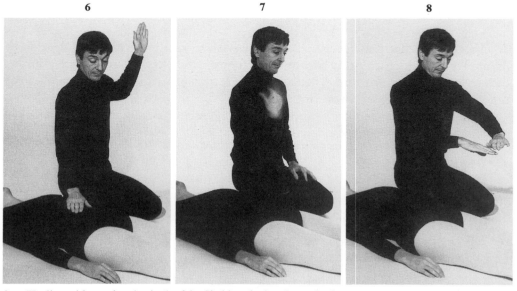

6	7	8
3c. Healing with one hand raised	3d. Shaking the hand to refresh	3d. Brushing the hands to refresh

natural, peaceful breathing. Begin with the hands in the Unifying Position, to unify energies.

c. Use one hand for healing and rest the other hand in the lap. You may also hold the other hand up or down to draw in energy from the sky or the earth, or alternate with resting the hand.

d. The giver extends on palm and places it over the selected organ. Giver and receiver breathe together. The giver may chant if desired. Visualization of healing images may be used. Allow energy to flow, and continue several minutes or longer. Notice fluctuations in energy and if discomfort arises, remove the hands, rest and refresh before resuming.

e. When the giver and receiver feel that enough practice has been done, remove the hands, smooth down the body's energy, and relax.

4. Back-and-Front Care for One Organ. If we wish to intensify the energy flow to a certain organ, front-and-back care is helpful. Placing the palm on the front and back sides of the organ sets up an energy flow between the palms, creating a more energizing, vitalizing effect. Generally, the giver's stronger hand is placed on the side to which you wish to draw more healing power.

a. The receiver takes the Seiza or other straight, comfortable sitting position, breathing peacefully, eyes closed or partly open. Hands may be folded in the lap, or held in the Unifying Position for more energy, if desired.

b. The giver sits at the side and begins with hands in the Unifying Position, with natural breathing following that of the receiver. The giver may chant if desired.

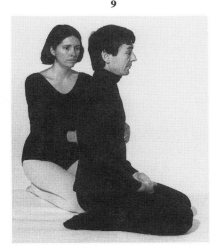

9

4c. Palm healing one organ front and back

During Back and Front Care, energy flows between the palms, passing through the receiver's body and circulating through the organs.

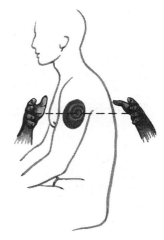

c. The giver extends one palm to the front, and the other palm to the back position at the selected organ. Breathe fully and naturally, chanting if desired. Allow energy to flow two to three minutes, using visualization if you wish.

d. Remove the hands, smooth down the energy if desired, and relax.

Complementary and Antagonistic Organ Relationships

Our organs work in pairs in terms of their functions. Within each pair, one organ is more yin, the other more yang; their functions are complementary or antagonistic, each organ working in cooperation with its partner. The list below shows the major pairs of organs. Notice that organs that have a yang structure have a yin energy flow and vice versa. This is because a yin energy flow *produces* a yang structure in physical form, and vice versa.

In palm healing we are generally dealing with energy flow, so that even though the liver is a yang organ by structure, for example, in order to nourish its energy, we use more yin, Earth's force. We do this through palm healing exercises geared to more upward movement, use of yin breathing, and other yin factors. This subject will be discussed in more detail in Chapter 8.

The condition of each organ closely influences that of its partner. They share a closely coordinated energy flow. Thus, palm healing given to one organ is also reflected in its complementary/antagonistic partner.

Yang organs by structure, having more yin energy flow	*Yin organs by structure, having more yang energy flow*
Lungs	Large Intestine
Heart	Small Intestine
Kidneys	Bladder
Spleen/Pancreas	Stomach
Liver	Gallbladder

10   5c.

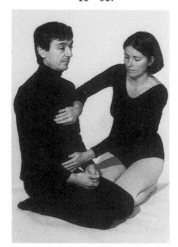

Complementary healing of the heart and small intestine is shown.

5. Palm Healing Using Complementary Organs. Palm healing care given to two complementary organs together, produces an especially strong flow of energy which benefits both organs.

   a. The receiver sits or lies down, eyes closed or partly open, hands relaxed or in the Unifying Position. Breathing is natural and peaceful.

   b. The giver sits to the side, hands in the Unifying Position, also with peaceful, natural breathing.

   c. The giver places one palm on an organ, and the other on its complementary partner. (The stronger hand can be on the organ which needs the most care.) In this exercise we are using positions on the front of the body, except for the kidneys, which are located more toward the back. Synchronize breathing and allow energy to flow two to three minutes, chanting if desired. The giver may touch the receiver, or may hold the palms 1/2 to 1 inch away, as desired.

d.   When the two organs feel energized, remove hands and relax.

Suggested Complementary Organ Combinations

Right Lung . . . . Left Side of Large Intestine
Left Lung . . . . Right Side of Large Intestine
Heart . . . . Small Intestine
Center Back between Kidneys . . . . Bladder
Right Kidney. . . . . Bladder
Left Kidney . . . . Bladder
Stomach . . . . Spleen/Pancreas
      etc.

6.   Back-Front Care for Complementary Organs.

An even stronger, more polarized energy flow may be set up between two complementary organs when one is touched at the front position while the other is touched at the back position. Generally, the organ that is touched at the front position receives more energy, and the stronger hand is placed at this location. (One exception would be the kidneys. Since they are located more toward the back, in order to give more energy to the kidneys, the stronger hand may be placed at the back position.) The other organ then acts in a more complementary fashion, however, both organs are energized and benefit from this exercise.

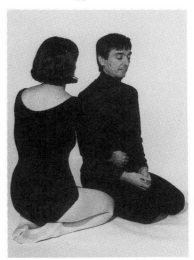

11   6b.

Back and front healing of complementary organs. In this example, Pauline's stronger hand is placed on the front of Steve's small intestine while her other hand is on the back of his heart area.

a.   The receiver sits straight and comfortably, eyes closed or partly open, breathing naturally, hands in the lap or in the Unifying Position. The giver sits to the side and also begins with hands in the Unifying Position.

b.   The giver places one hand on the front position of one organ, and the other hand on the back position of the complementary organ. Synchronize breathing with the receiver, chanting if desired, and allow energy to flow two to three minutes.

c.   Remove the hands and relax.

Head-Body Relationships

The head is a compact version of the body, as we have studied briefly in Chapter 2. Each area of the head and each facial feature corresponds to an organ of the body. Palm healing care given to the head or face not only improves that area itself, but also aids the organs that correspond to it in the lower body. The accompanying illustrations show which areas of the head and face relate to which bodily organs, and the list describes these in detail.

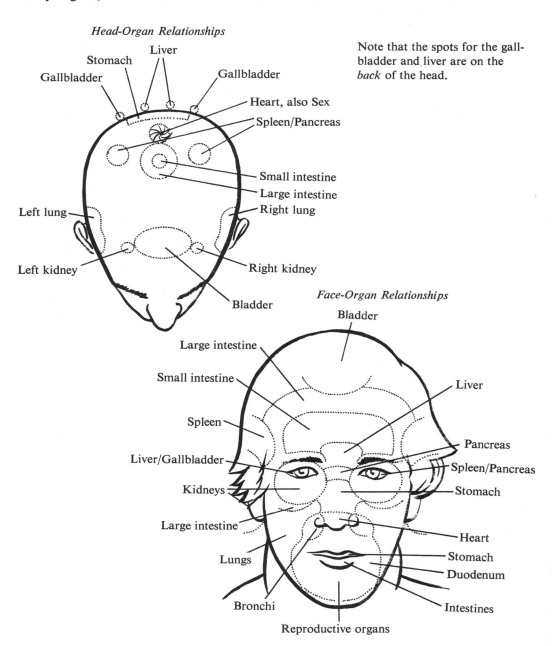

Head-Organ Relationships

Note that the spots for the gallbladder and liver are on the *back* of the head.

Face-Organ Relationships

The Organs and Their Corresponding Areas on the Head and Face

Organ	Facial Feature(s)	Area of Head
Lungs	Opposite cheeks	Sides of upper forehead
Large Intestine	Mouth (lower lip and cheek	Circular area at top of head around small-intestine area
Heart	Tip of nose	Central spiral near top of head
Small Intestine	Mouth and area below eyes (lower than eyelids)	Small circular spot at top of headlids
Spleen, Pancreas	Left eye and root of nose (upper bridge)	Two small circular spots at left and right on top of head
Stomach	Pillar of nose and upper lip	Wide, flat region at upper back part of head
Liver	Eyes, especially right eye; also lower forehead between eyebrows	Two small circular spots at middle back of head, just below stomach area and to left and right of center line
Gallbladder	At ends of eyebrows	Two small circular spots at middle back of head, left and right of liver areas
Kidneys	Left ear—left kidney; right ear—right kidney; also around eyes	Two small circular spots at upper forehead, right and left of center. Right spot—left kidney, left spot—right kidney.
Bladder	Forehead	Large area at center of upper forehead
Reproductive organs (give palm-healing care at base of spine and abdomen)	Around mouth, lower part of cheek and jaw	Same as heart area: hair spiral near top of head

7. Palm Healing for the Face and Head. In this exercise, we give palm healing care to benefit parts of the face and head. We follow the procedure outlined for giving palm healing care to organs, Exercises 1, 2, and 3. If chanting, the sound "Mmmm" is especially helpful for the head region. Notice that "Mmmm" is a very compact sound and is nourishing for the head, which is a very compact part of the body. Suggestions for giving palm healing care to various parts of the face and head are listed below. Some suggestions are for using one hand, and some are for using two hands in a complementary fashion.

Area Needing Care	Suggested Palm Positions
Eyes	One hand: on eye needing care, center of palm directly over the eye Two hands: one hand on one eye, the other on the back of the head (opposite side of head), or on the other eye
Ears	One hand: center of palm on ear needing care Two hands: one hand on the one ear, the other on the other ear

Sinus	One hand: on uncomfortable area
	Two hands: one hand on uncomfortable area, the other on the opposite side of the face, or on the back of the head
Cheeks	One hand on each cheek
Jaws	One hand on each side of the jaw
Mouth	One hand: on the mouth, gently
	Two hands: one on the mouth, the other on the root of the nose between the eyebrows.
Head	Sides of head: one palm on each side.
	Top of head: one hand on top, the other on the back base of the skull
	Top of head: one hand on top, the other on the throat just below the jaw
	Forehead or back of head: one hand on each area

12   13   14

7.   Self-care for jaws

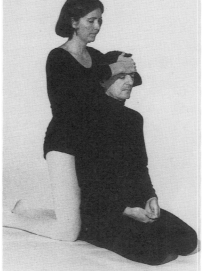

7.   Self-care, front and back of head

7.   Partner care, front and back of head

8. Palm Healing Care Using Facial Features and Organs. This exercise utilizes the natural energy flow that exists between bodily organs and the facial features that correspond with them. It is practiced in the same way as Exercise 5 for Complementary Organs—one hand on the organ, the other hand on the facial feature that corresponds. Both the organ and the facial feature are energized. Refer to the list of corresponding organs and facial features for examples.

- To draw more energy to the bodily organ, chant a fuller sound such as "Ah," "A-U-M," or "Su," and use the stronger hand on the organ.
- To draw more energy to the facial feature, chant the compacted "Mmmm" sound, and use the stronger hand there.

Use the same sequence of steps as described in Exercise 5, remembering that full, natural breathing, synchronized between giver and receiver, aids in promoting good energy flow.

a. The receiver sits or lies down comfortably and the giver sits at the side. Eyes may be closed or partly open, hands in the lap or in the Unifying Position.

b. The giver places one hand on the organ, the other hand on the corresponding facial feature. Hold this position two to three minutes, breathing naturally and chanting if desired, either touching or holding the palm 1/2 to 1 inch away.

15 8b.

16 8b.

Self-care of spleen and left eye

Self-care of stomach and bridge of nose

c. Lower the hands and relax.

9. Palm Healing Care Using Organs and Corresponding Head Areas. This exercise is done in the same way as Exercise 8, but instead of using facial features, we use the areas on the head corresponding with the internal organs. Notice any differences in effect between Exercises 8 and 9.

17 9. Heart-head spiral

18

10. Palm Healing Care Using Face and Head Areas. This exercise is helpful when we wish to concentrate more energy in the head. The specific area of the face and of the head and brain is helped, strengthening their functions. This also serves to clarify and regulate brain functions. You may do this exercise for yourself, or for another person. Simply place one hand on the facial feature, and the other hand on the part of the head that is related. If chanting is desired, the more contracted sounds "Mmmm" or Iiii" (Eeee) may be used to bring more energy to the head.

10. Left ear and left upper forehead

A secondary result of this exercise is to bring a gentle, beneficial influence to the related bodily organ. If you wish to accentuate this influence, chant a more yang, full sound such as "Su," "Ah," or "Toh," although other palm healing exercises relate more directly to the bodily organs.

Refer to the list of face and head areas for examples to practice. The list below gives some ideas to begin with.

One hand on:	Other hand on:	Helps:	Also helps:
Tip of nose	Hair spiral	Those areas	Heart
Mouth, especially upper lip	Top center of head	Those areas	Small Intestine
Left ear	Left top forehead	Those areas	Left kidney
Right eye	Back of head near center middle	Those areas	Liver

Beneficial Times of Day

Throughout the day, the flow of energy between the sky and the earth varies from hour to hour. The different organs, each having a slightly different proportion of Heaven's and Earth's energy flow, are more energized at different times of day or night. To give maximum benefit to a certain organ, we can apply palm healing care at the time of day when it is naturally the most energized.

The list that follows shows the times of day when the various organs are more active. When it is not possible to give palm healing at the exact time (such as 3:00 to 5:00 A.M.), you can apply palm healing several hours in advance. For example, give palm healing in the morning for organs listed from 5 A.M. to Noon, in the afternoon for those listed from Noon to 6 or 7 P.M., and in the evening for those listed after 7 or 9 P.M.

For additional benefit, face in the appropriate direction in relation to the rising or setting sun as described in Chapter 3.

Please note that this is a refinement for palm healing practice, and care may be given to any organ at any time with beneficial results.

Times of Day Each Organ Is More Activated

5–7 A.M.	Large Intestine
7–9 A.M.	Stomach
9–11 A.M.	Spleen/Pancreas
11 A.M.–1 P.M.	Heart
1–3 P.M.	Small Intestine
3–5 P.M.	Bladder
5–7 P.M.	Kidneys
7–9 P.M.	Heart Governor (Pericardium)
9–11 P.M.	Triple Heater
11 P.M.–1 A.M.	Gallbladder
1–3 A.M.	Liver
3–5 A.M.	Lungs

Times of Year. Further studies in Oriental medicine that can be helpful for our palm healing practice include seasonal changes in energy flow. As the type of energy changes from one season to the next, the various organs are affected in different ways and are more activated in certain seasons. In the list above, generally substitute spring for morning, summer for noon, autumn for sunset, and winter for late evening. It is possible for us to make the most progress in helping a certain organ in its active season, although we can give benefits at any time of year.

Chapter 7

Using the Meridians and Points for Healing

The meridians are pathways taken by energy flowing through our body. Branching out from the spiritual channel, energy flows along the meridian pathways through every part of the body, nourishing us with vital force. The points, located along the meridians, serve as places where energy may enter and leave the meridian flow. Each meridian is associated with specific bodily organs and functions, and each point also has specific functions. By giving palm healing care to the meridians and points, we can benefit particular organs and body functions as needed.

In general, meridians connected with upper-body organs run through the arms, and those connected with lower-body organs run through the legs. A general overview of our meridian system is shown in Chapter 2, and more detailed meridian maps are presented here. Our energy structure has a great natural simplicity, and yet to fully understand it required years of study. We recommend taking classes and studying books on Oriental medicine for further information.

1.   Locating the Meridians.   We use palm healing to encourage the flow of energy through our meridians, thus improving our total health condition. In this exercise we locate and trace the pathways of the meridians, sensing the energy flow. At the same time, we strengthen the energy flowing through the meridians. We use the breath, inhaling and exhaling as described to assist in this process. The meridian maps show the approximate location of each meridian, but this may vary slightly from person to person.

This exercise is designed for two persons, but may also be done alone, to notice and give energy care to our own meridians.

1   1a.   Starting posture

a. The receiver may sit or lie down comfortably, breathing naturally. Eyes may be closed or partly open, hands relaxed, folded or in the Unifying Position if desired. The giver sits at the side and begins with hands in the Unifying Position, also breathing peacefully and naturally.

b. The giver uses one hand to sense the meridians, while the other hand rests in the lap (or may be raised or lowered to bring in Heaven's or Earth's force). To check the meridian, use the central palm point and/or the spiral point near the

103

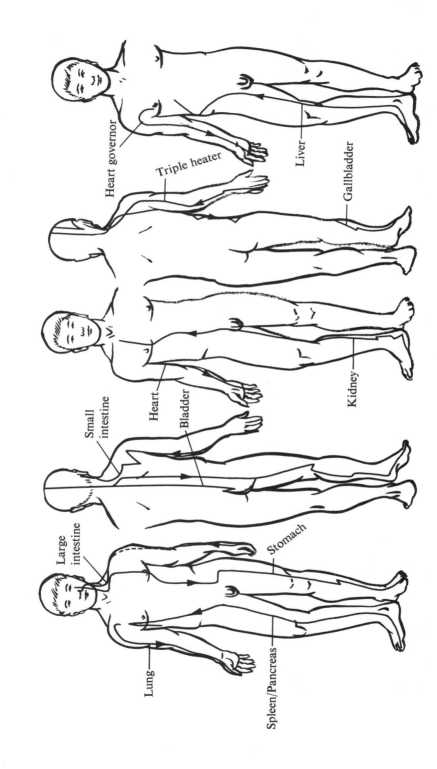

The Major Meridians with Direction of Flow

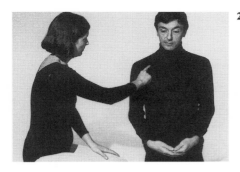

2 1d. Beginning point of meridian. In this photo, it is the Bo point of the Heart Meridian.

3 1f.

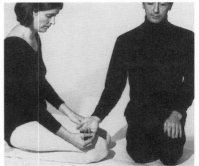

End point of meridian. Here it is the Sei point of the Heart Meridian.

end of the thumb, index, or middle finger. Eyes may be open, but it is very interesting to try this exercise with eyes closed, just following your true sensations of energy rather than tracing the "expected" meridian location from the maps.

c. The giver breathes at the same time as the receiver, following the receiver's breathing speed, inhaling and exhaling together. If desired, the giver may chant on the exhalation and the balanced sound "Su" may be used, or another sound as desired.

d. The giver begins by placing the hand (using the palm or spiral point) at the beginning point of the meridian. Hold the palm at that point while you breathe in, not touching the body.

e. While you exhale, slowly move the hand along the meridian a few inches. The hand is held 1/2 to 1 inch above the surface of the body. When you inhale, stop and hold the hand steady at that place.

f. Exhale again, moving the hand further along the meridian. Stop and inhale again. Continue this way until you have reached the end point of the meridian. Hold the hand steady there for a moment, then gently lift it off.

g. Try several meridians in this manner.

h. Smooth down the body's energy with one or both palms to finish and relax.

Variations of Exercise 1. There are quite a number of ways to work with the meridians. Some variations on the above exercise are listed below.

- Moving the finger on the exhalation emphasizes contracting, yang energy or Heaven's force. If you wish to emphasize the opposite—expanding, yin energy or Earth's force—move your finger on the inhalation, and rest during the exhalation.

- Note that some meridians have a yin, upward direction of energy flow, and others have a yang, downward direction of flow. To refine this meridian exercise, move your finger in this direction of flow and use the inhalation to move your finger for the yin meridians, and the exhalation to move your finger for the yang meridians.

- Try going through the entire meridian cycle; the twelve major meridians naturally flow into each other. Go from one to the next: Lung–Large Intestine–

Stomach–Spleen/Pancreas–Heart–Small Intestine–Bladder–Kidneys–Heart Governor–Triple Heater–Gallbladder–Liver.

- Try a simplified version of this exercise. Disregarding direction of meridian flow and forgetting about moving and stopping your hand, just breathe peacefully and naturally and slowly, while gently and steadily moving your hand along the meridian.

Heart-of-Hand and Heart-of-Foot Points

Four of the most important points are the centers of the palms and soles of the feet. The Heart-of-Hand points in the center of the palms are related to the intestines, the heart, and the Triple Heater, and help to regulate whole-body metabolism. The Heart-of-Foot points in the center of the soles of the feet are related to the kidneys, digestive, excretory, and reproductive functions. We use these four points to stimulate energy flow through the meridians for the whole body. The Heart-of-Hand points are the same as the central-palm area used when giving Palm healing.

Heart-of-Hand and Heart-of-Foot Points

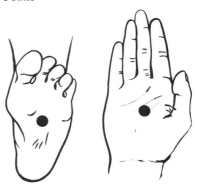

2. **Palm Healing Using the Heart-of-Hand and Heart-of-Foot Points.**
    a. The receiver sits in the Seiza or other comfortable, straight posture; the giver may stand behind or sit in front of the receiver as desired. Both begin with hands in the Unifying Position, breathing naturally, eyes closed or partly open. This exercise may be done silently, or the giver may chant, or—for more energy—both giver and receiver may chant "Su" or "A-U-M."

4

5

6

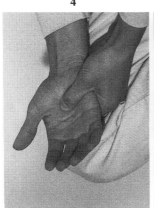

Heart-of-hand point demonstrated by Diane

Heart-of-foot point demonstrated by Diane

2b. Thumbs on the heart-of-hand points

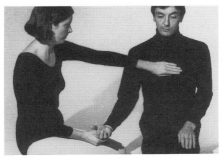

7   2c.   Heart and heart-of-hand

b. The giver extends both hands and gently graps the receiver's hands, placing the thumb spiral on the receiver's Heart-of-Hand points. If the giver is standing behind, the receiver's hands may be held up to about shoulder level, in a relaxed fashion. Breathe in synchronization fully and nsturally, chanting if desired, two to three minutes. Lower the hands and relax.

c. The giver next sits at the receiver's side, hands in the Unifying Position. The giver extends one palm to cover the heart region, and with the other hand, takes the receiver's hand and places the thumb spiral on one Heart-of-Hand. Breathe together, as above, with chanting if desired.

d. Keeping one palm on the Heart-of-Hand, the giver moves the other palm to the stomach region and proceeds as in step *c*.

e. The giver keeps one palm on the Heart-of-Hand, and moves the other palm to the hara, and proceeds as above. Then relax.

f. Next we go to the Heart-of-Foot points. The receiver lies down comfortably on the stomach, soles of the feet facing up. (It is also possible to do this exercise sitting up if preferred.) The giver sits near the feet and begins with hands in the Unifying Position for a moment to unify energies. The receiver breathes naturally and peacefully.

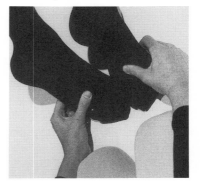

8   2g.   Thumbs on the heart-of-foot points

g. The giver extends the hands and gently grasps the receiver's feet, gently touching the thumb spirals to the Heart-of-Foot points. Breathe together, chanting if desired, allowing energy to flow two to three minutes.

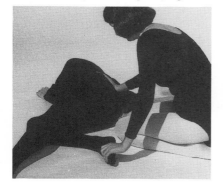

9   2h.   Kidney and foot point, leg bent

h. The giver moves to the side and sits near the receiver's knee area. The giver places the thumb spiral on the Heart-of-Foot point of one of the receiver's feet. The other palm is placed on the receiver's kidney (same side). To reach both locations, the receiver's leg may have to bend and rest in a comfortable bent position. Breathe together, chanting if desired, two to three minutes, allowing energy to flow.

i. Continuing to hold one hand on the Heart-of-Foot point, the giver moves the other hand to the base of the spine to benefit

the bladder and reproductive organs.
Hold two to three minutes as above,
then remove the hands.

j. Use one or both palms held 1 to 2 inches
away to gently smooth the whole body's
energy. Then relax.

11 2i.

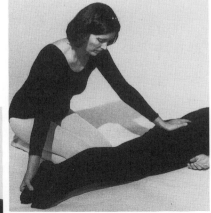

One foot point and base of spine

10 2h.

Kidney and foot point,
a different position

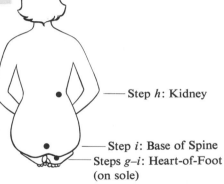

Steps c–e:
Heart-of-Hand——
(on palm)

———Step c: Heart
——Step d: Stomach
———Step e: Hara

Steps c–e: One hand touching the Heart-
of-Hand, while the other hand touches
the points illustrated.

———Step h: Kidney

———Step i: Base of Spine
——Steps g–i: Heart-of-Foot
(on sole)

Steps g–i: One hand touches the
Heart-of-Foot, while the other hand
touches the points illustrated. Then
repeat these steps using the foot and
kidney of the other side.

Variations on Exercise 2.   This exercise shows a comprehensive use of the
heart-of-Hand and Heart-of-Foot points. Try the following variations as well:

• For a more brief exercise, use just one of the positions described, covering
only one region of the body in the session.

• For a more comprehensive exercise, to give more care to upper-body energy,
repeat the exercise steps c, d, and e on both left and right sides, first with
the receiver's right Heart-of-Hand, then with the left.

• For a more comprehensive exercise emphasizing more care to the lower body,
repeat steps h and i on both sides, first with the receiver's right Heart-of-
Foot points, then with the left.

Five Kinds of Points

The more than 360 points located along our meridians may be classified in a number of ways. Here we would like to introduce five major categories of points which can be used in palm healing exercises. Generally speaking, any of the points that are studied in connection with acupuncture or shiatsu massage, may also be incorporated into palm healing exercises. As described in the foregoing exercise, we touch the points gently with the center of our palm, thumb, or finger spiral, thus stimulating or regulating the flow of energy.

The five types points we are discussing are located at different segments of each meridian and represent different functions in energy flow:

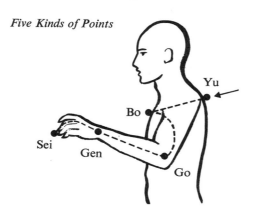

Five Kinds of Points

Yu points, located on the back, also called "Entering Points"; energy enters here to go toward the internal organs.

Bo points, located on the front of the body, also called "Gathering Points"; energy that has flowed through the organs comes out and gathers here to go toward the arm and leg meridians.

Go points, located near the elbows and knees, along the arm and leg meridians, also known as "Meeting of Energy Points"; help to regulate the flow of energy through the meridians.

Gen points, also called "Balancing Points"; are located near the wrists and ankles and function as the midpoints of the meridian in terms of the number of sections on the arm or leg.

● *Sei* points are located at the ends of the fingers and toes, and are also called "Well" or "Spring Point"; because here, energy bubbles out from the meridians like water from a spring or well. From the Sei points, energy leaves one meridian and goes toward the next meridian.

Sei (Well) Points. These points are frequently used in palm healing as well as in shiatsu massage, to activate the energy flow through the related meridians,

Meridian for:	Sei-Point Location:	Meridian for:	Sei-Point Location:
Lung	Thumb	Kidney	Heart-of-Foot
Large Intestine	Index finger, back	Spleen/Pancreas	Big toe (outside)
Heart Governor	Middle finger	Liver	Big toe (inside)
Triple Heater	Fourth finger, back	Stomach	Second and third toes
Heart	Little finger	Gallbladder	Fourth toe
Small Intestine	Little finger, back	Bladder	Little toe

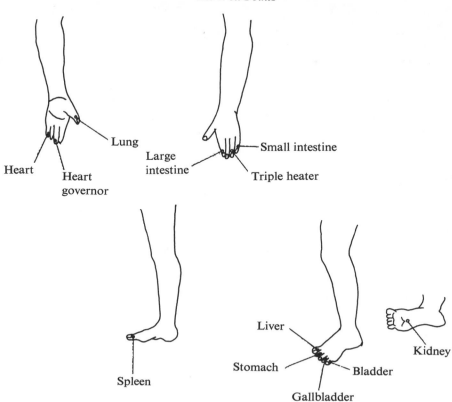

organs, and complementary organs. The locations of the Sei (Well) Points are as follows. Please see the accompanying illustrations as well.

In order to activate the whole upper-body region, we can simply grasp all fingertips. To active the whole lower-body region, grasp all toes, for a quick general method.

12 3b.

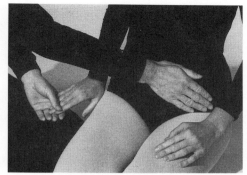

Organ and Sei point. Here, it is the descending colon.

3. Palm Healing for Internal Organs Using the Sei (Well) Points.

a. The receiver sits down or lies comfortably, eyes closed or half open, breathing naturally. The giver sits at the side, also breathing naturally and peacefully, and may begin synchronizing with the receiver's breathing speed. Chanting may be added if desired.

b. The giver places one hand on the organ needing care, and places the thumb spiral of the other hand on the corresponding Sei point of the receiver's hand or foot. If it is a foot point, you may need to ask the receiver to bend the leg in a comfortable, relaxed fashion.

c.   Breathing naturally (and perhaps chanting), keep this position and allow energy to flow two to three minutes or as desired.

d.   Change to the opposite side and repeat.

e.   Try several organs and their Sei points. Notice the type of energy flow for each.

f.   Remove the hands and relax.

As a variation in this exercise, try holding one hand on each Sei point (two sides) without touching the organ itself.

Yu (Entering) Points.   These points, where energy flows into the beginning of the meridian, are located on the back, on the Bladder Meridian which runs on both sides of the spine. Note that there are two Yu points for each organ, one on the left, the other on the right side of the spine. Stimulation of the Yu points can send increased energy flowing through the meridians and organs.

Yu-Entering and Bo-Gathering Points

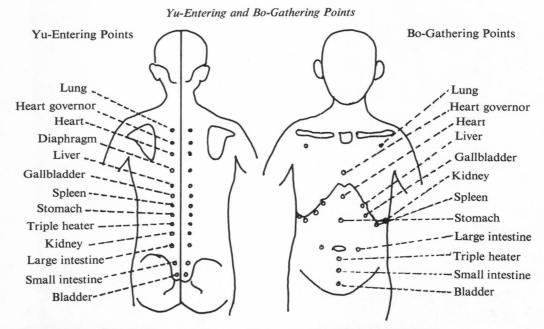

Yu-Entering Points | Bo-Gathering Points

Lung
Heart governor
Heart
Diaphragm
Liver
Gallbladder
Spleen
Stomach
Triple heater
Kidney
Large intestine
Small intestine
Bladder

Lung
Heart governor
Heart
Liver
Gallbladder
Kidney
Spleen
Stomach
Large intestine
Triple heater
Small intestine
Bladder

4.   Palm Healing for Internal Organs Using the Yu (Entering) Points.

a.   The receiver sits in the Seiza or other position; the giver sits at the side. Both breathe naturally and peacefully together, chanting if desired. The receiver may have the hands in the lap, or in the Unifying Position.

b.   The giver places one hand on the organ needing care, and the other hand touches the two Yu points corresponding to that organ, using the spirals of the thumb and index finger. Allow energy to flow two to three minutes.

c.   Try other organ and Yu-point pairs, noticing the energy differences.

d.   Remove the hands and relax.

As a variation to this exercise, try the Yu-points alone. Sit at the receiver's back and select one set of points—for example, the Lung Yu-points. Touch each Yu point with one thumb spiral.

13 4b.

Organ and Yu points. Steve places one hand on the liver while touching the two Liver Yu points with the other hand.

5. Palm Healing Using Yu and Sei Points.   In this exercise we stimulate the beginning (Yu) and ending (Sei) points of one meridian in order to accelerate and strengthen the energy flow.

a.   The receiver and giver sit in the Seiza or other position, breathing peacefully and naturally at the same speed (giver follows receiver's speed). The receiver's hands may be in the lap, or in the Unifying Position. The giver sits to the side.

b.   Selecting one meridian, the giver touches one thumb spiral to the Sei point at the end of the finger or toe, and the thumb and index finger spirals of the other hand to the two Yu points on the back for the same meridian. Allow energy to flow two to three minutes, chanting if desired.

c.   Remove the hands and relax.

14 5b.

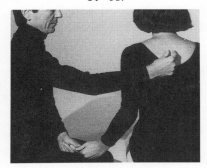

Steve uses one thumb and index finger on the two Lung Yu points, while touching the Lung Sei point with the other hand.

Bo (Gathering) Points.   Energy which has entered the meridian at the Yu points and circulated through the internal organs, then exits at the Bo points on the front of the body. Energy gathers there and then streams out along the meridians of the arms or legs. The Bo points, like the Yu points, are in pairs on the right and left sides of the torso and are located as shown in the accompanying illustration.

6. Palm Healing Using Bo-points and Yu-points Together.   The Bo-points and Yu-points are in a complementary relationship—back versus front, entering versus exiting and gathering. Using them together in healing helps to strengthen the energy flow back and front through the organs.

a.   The receiver and giver sit in the Seiza or other posture, breathing in synchronization peacefully and naturally. The receiver may place the hands in the lap, or in the Unifying Position.

b.   The giver places one thumb spiral on the front

15 6b.

One hand on the Stomach Bo point, using index finger, and the other touching the Stomach Yu points in back

Bo point, and the thumb and index spirals of the other hand on the corresponding Yu points. (If possible, reach both Bo points in front with the thumb and index finger of one hand.)

c.   Giver and receiver breathe nsturally, chanting if desired, allowing energy to flow two to three minutes.

d.   Try several sets of Yu and Bo points.

e.   Remove the hands, finalize, and relax.

Gen (Balancing) Points.   Located near the wrists and ankles, the Gen points act as the midpoint of each meridian, not in terms of inches, but in terms of the number of sections of the arm or leg. Due to their location, the Gen points function as a balancing location, like the fulcrum of a seesaw. Their locations are shown in the accompanying illustration.

One frequently used Gen point is called *Gō-Koku*, on the Large Intestine Meridian. Located on the hand in the depressed area between the thumb and index finger,

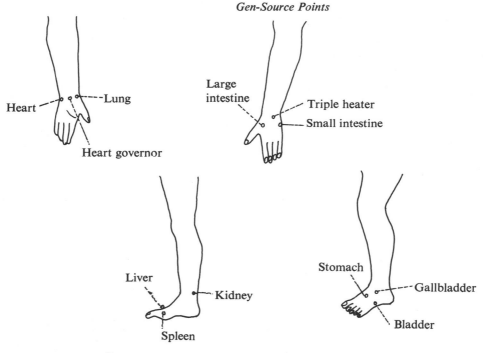

Gen-Source Points

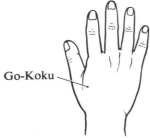

but back toward the wrist (see drawing), Gō-Koku influences the intestines and digestive function when stimulated.

7.   Palm Healing with Gen Points.   The Gen (Balancing) points assist in harmonizing and equalizing the flow of energy through the meridians so that it is well-balanced and regulated.

a. The receiver may sit or lie down comfortably and the giver sits at the side. Both breathe naturally and may chant if desired. Eyes may be closed or lightly open.

b. The giver places the stronger hand on the selected organ, and the thumb spiral of the other hand gently holds the Gen point corresponding to that organ. Hold two to three minutes or as desired, breathing peacefully or chanting.

c. Repeat on the other side.

d. Try several other organs and their Gen points.

e. Remove the hands, finalize, and relax.

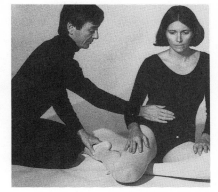

16 7b.

This example shows palm healing for the liver and its Gen point near the ankle.

Go (Meeting) Points. Located near the elbows and knees, the Go points are known as "Meeting of Energy." Their function is to activate the energy as it progresses through the meridian. The energy is encouraged along in a smooth, activat-

Go-Meeting Points

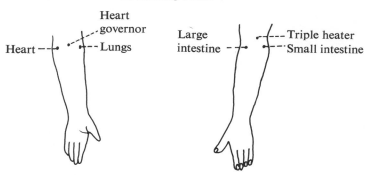

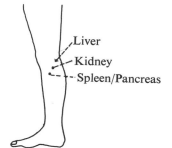

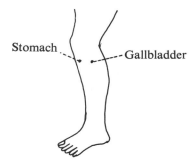

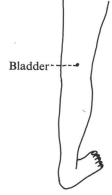

ing manner as though joining energies of all parts of the meridian. The Go point locations are shown in the accompanying illustration.

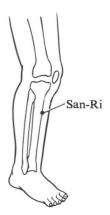

One well-known Go point is called *San-Ri*. This is on the Stomach Meridian, located on the outside of the leg, about three-fingers width down from the knee on the bony ridge. (See drawing.) It is traditionally said that stimulation of this point helps preserve health and longevity. When long trips were accomplished primarily by walking, travelers made sure to stimulate San-Ri before setting out on an important journey. This point is also used traditionally for stomach disorders and for digestive and respiratory organs in general.

8. Palm Healing for the Internal Organs Using the Go-Points.

Using the Go points in palm healing has the effect of accelerating or urging the flow of energy through the meridian in a subtle but powerful manner. This helps to draw stagnated energy out of the related organs and draw in a flow of fresh energy.

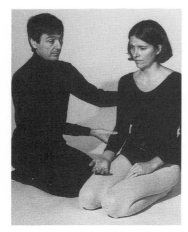

17 8b.

One hand on the back of the lung, the other on the Lung Go point near the elbow

   a.   The receiver may lie down or sit comfortably and the giver sits at the side. Both breathe naturally and peacefully, eyes closed or gently open.

   b.   The giver places one hand on the organ needing care, and touches the thumb spiral of the other hand to the Go point that corresponds. Generally, it is more effective to use the opposite side of the body from the elbow or knee area you are touching. Breathe together, chanting if desired, allowing energy to flow two to three minutes or more.

   c.   Try several other organs and their corresponding Go points.

   d.   Remove the hands, finalize, and relax.

Additional Uses of Points in Palm Healing.   In addition to the exercises in Chapter 7, there are many ways to use points in palm healing. The Yu, Bo, Sei, Gen, and Go points may be used alone, in combination with organs, with other points, and in combination with complementary organs. By studying Oriental medicine theory in more detail, we can learn other important points and their uses, and incorporate these in palm healing practice. The exercises in this chapter show some of the primary uses of points in palm healing; please experiment, study, and discover more.

Chapter 8
Improving Your Technique

After learning basic palm healing exercises, you may want to add some refinements to improve your technique. While these methods are optional, they can be helpful for increasing the effectiveness of palm healing care. In this chapter we will discuss some special uses of sound, breathing, hand movements, and other suggestions for refining palm healing technique. Of course, it is important that these methods be used in a good, basic palm healing practice as described in the first few chapters of this book.

In order to see the effect of each method clearly, it is not a good idea to try them all in one session, but to use each one singly in a simple manner. In this way you can experience the effect of each variable as you introduce it into your practice of palm healing. Experience each technique from both angles—giver and receiver. After clearly understanding the effect of each technique, it is possible to combine the techniques in palm healing exercises in a beneficial manner.

Sound

Sound waves are vibrations created by the movement of objects. These vibrations travel through the air and when they enter our inner ear, we interpret these vibrations as sound. Each sound has a different vibratory rate—those that vibrate at a slower speed produce lower, more relaxed sounds; those that vibrate at a faster speed produce higher, tighter sounds. These sounds have varying yin and yang qualities, as shown in the following list:

Sound	Yin or Yang Quality
Mmm	tight, yang
Iii ("eee")	tight, yang
Ehhh	in-between
Uuu (like "boo")	middle, balanced
Ooooh (like "toe")	more open, in-between
Ahhh	open, yin

We can use this knowledge of yin and yang sounds in healing. For example, if we are too yin, loose and relaxed, we can chant or sing a yang sound, which creates a tight, yang vibration that can help to influence our condition toward a more balanced state. If we are too yang, tight and tense, a more yin, relaxed sound can be helpful. A balanced sound such as "Uuuu" tends to bring our condition toward the center as well.

We can use sounds to help our condition as a whole, or we can chant a certain

116

sound to help a specific organ. Yin or yang breathing can be used at the same time for additional effect, together with palm healing exercises.

The head is a tight, compact part of the body and is nourished by more closed, yang sounds. The lower body is more expanded and loose, and is nourished by more yin, open sounds. The middle part of the body is more balanced, and is nourished by more middle sounds. Consequently, the different regions of the body are generally nourished by the following sounds:

Sounds Corresponding to Approximate Body Regions

Sound	Region of Body Nourished
Mmm	Head region
Iii	Head region and upper throat
Ehh	Upper midsection
Uuu	Midsection
Oooh	Lower midsection
Ahhh	Lower body

Mmm, Iii

Iii

Ehh

Uuu

Oooh

Ahh

1. Using Sounds for Regions of the Body. We can use sound to give more strength to a certain part of the body as follows.

   a. While meditating, chant one sound ten to fifteen times, noticing what part of the body it vibrates the most. Then, do the same with the other sounds, one by one. You may hold your hand at different places on the body to detect the vibration.

   b. While giving palm healing to another person, chant a sound while holding your hand at the corresponding region of the body, to reinforce the energy flow at that place. You may also hold your hands front and back at that region.

   c. While practicing a complementary/antagonistic hand position, for example, one hand on the forehead and the other on the hara, chant the sound corresponding to the region you wish to energize the most. For example, in this case, if you wish to give more energy to the hara, chant "Ohhh" or "Ahhh." If you wish to benefit the head more, chant "Mmm" or "Iii."

1 1a.   **2** 1a.

Steve chants Uuu while placing his hand on the stomach.

Steve chants Iii and places his hand on his throat.

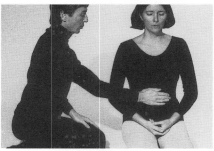

3 1b. Chanting Uuu while giving palm healing to the midsection

Sounds for Each Organ. Since each organ has a different proportion of yin and yang, Earth's and Heaven's energy flow, certain sounds benefit certain organs more than others, depending on their yin or yang qualities. Through many generations of experience, practitioners of traditional Oriental medicine arrived at the following understanding of specific sounds to benefit each organ.

Organ	Nourishing Sound	Organs	Nourishing Sound
Lungs	Ha	Large Intestine	Ah or Ho
Heart	Shi ("sheee")	Small Intestine	Toh or So
Spleen/Pancreas	Hi ("heee")	Stomach	Iii ("eee")
Kidneys	Ji ("geee")	Bladder	Bo or Bu
Liver	Ka or Kan	Gallbladder	Da

2. Using Sounds for Specific Organs. We can strengthen specific organs through using their corresponding sounds in a number of ways, such as:

a. While meditating, practicing palm healing, or Dō-In, chant the sound for the organ you wish to benefit. Chant ten to fifteen times, and place your palm on the corresponding organ if desired.

b. While giving palm healing care to another person, chant the appropriate sound while you place your hand on a certain organ.

c. While placing hands in a complementary fashion, such as one hand on the lung and the other hand on the large intestine, chant the sound for the organ to which you want to direct more energy. Your stronger hand may be placed on that organ as well.

4

5

6

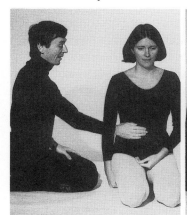

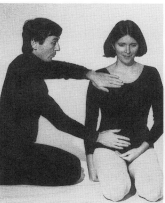

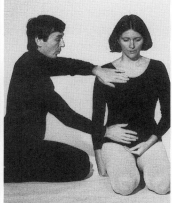

2b. Liver—Kaaa

2c. Ha for the lung, with complementary hand position, lung-large intestine

2c. Ho for the large intestine, with same complementary hand position

Quality of Sound. In addition to the sound chanted, the volume, pitch, and other qualities also help to create an effect that is more yin (loose, relaxed) or more yang (tense, tight).

Quality	More Yin	More Yang
Volume:	Quieter	Louder
Pitch:	Lower, bass	Higher, soprano
Speed:	Long, drawn-out	Short, quick
Articulation:	Soft, dull/muted	Sharp, distinct
Mood or intention:	Peaceful, soothing	Cheerful, bright

We can use these different qualities of sound during palm healing by varying the way we chant, sing, or clap our hands according to the needs of the situation. For example, a person who is very tight and tense (yang) would benefit more if the giver chants in a more yin manner (peaceful, softer sounds) while giving palm healing care. On the other hand, someone who is depressed, loose, and too yin, would be more helped by sounds that are made in a more yang way—more cheerful, quick, and distinct.

In both cases, the sounds should not be extreme. An overly yang sound may be too loud or harsh, an overly yin sound too soft or whining. They should be of a moderate, pleasant yin or yang quality.[1]

Breathing

In Chapter 3, we discussed yin and yang breathing methods. During palm healing for ourselves or for another person, we can use yin breathing to increase the upward flow of Earth's force and create a feeling of coolness, lightness, and detachment from the physical world. We can use yang breathing to strengthen the downward flow of Heaven's force, resulting in a feeling of warmth, contraction, and stability.

There are a number of ways we can use these special types of breathing during palm healing. For example, during meditation before palm healing, a yang person may use yin breathing to become more yin, and a yin person may use yang breathing to become more yang. While doing palm healing exercises, for someone who is too yin, yang breathing can be used to create more yang energy, and vice versa. Yin or yang breathing may also be used to draw attention to a certain organ. For an organ requiring more yin energy, use yin breathing while giving palm healing for that organ, or yang breathing for more yang energy.

Following are some exercises using the principles of breathing in palm healing.

Warm and Cold Breath.   Another way to create yin or yang qualities in breathing is to make our breath warm or cold. This can be used to create a more yin or yang influence during palm healing. To create a warm breath, hold your hand in front of your mouth and breathe out slowly with the sound "Haaa." The mouth is half open. On your hand, feel the effect of warmth. Next, to produce a cold breath, again hold your hand in front of your mouth and breathe out slowly form-

---

[1] For additional uses of sound, refer to *The Book of Dō-In* by Michio Kushi.

ing the mouth into the sound "Whooo." The mouth is contracted. Feel the effect of coolness on your hand, like a cool breeze.

The yang, warm breath, when given to your hand, causes your hand to relax. Yang produces yin relaxation. The cool, yin breath, when given to the hand, causes the hand to contract more. Yin produces yang contraction when it is externally applied in this manner. (Note that yin breathing, when done internally or to move *energy*, results in a more yin *energetic* effect, and yang breathing results in a yang *energetic* effect, whereas the externally applied warm or cool breath is affecting the physical *structures* of muscles and tissue.)

1. Relaxation Exercise Using Warm Breath

a. The receiver lies down comfortably, face down, or may sit if desired. The giver sits at the side. Both breathe naturally and peacefully. Eyes may be closed or gently open.

b. The giver encourages the receiver to stretch out and relax; gently extend the head-neck region upward, gently bouncing the head to encourage it to be more loose.

7 1b. Extend head and neck.

c. Gently stretch the arms and legs outward and downward in the same manner.

d. The giver next holds the palms about 1 inch above the body, and begins at the back of the neck, running the palms up toward the top of the head several times. Then, begin at the back of the neck again, running the palms down the arms several times. Then, begin at the back of the neck and run the

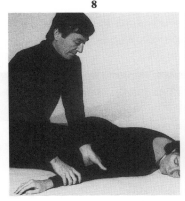

8

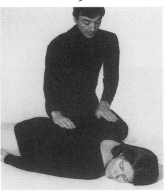

9

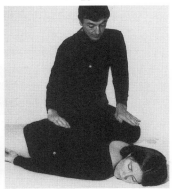

10

1c. Stretch arms and legs.   1d. Run palms down spine.   1d. Run palms from inside out.

palms down the spine several times. Next, begin at the top of the legs and run the palms down the legs to the toes several times. This encourages a relaxed, outward energy flow.

11 1e. Pinch fingertips outsward.   **12** 1f. Apply warm breach to back of neck.

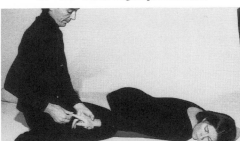
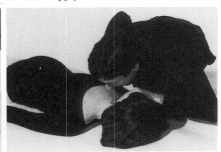

e. Fingertips and toes may be gently pinched in an outward direction.

f. At the back of the neck, apply a warm, yang breath (Haaa . . . Haaa) several times. This causes a yin reaction in the main point of the nervous system, resulting in relaxation. For best results, giver and receiver should exhale at the same time while the giver chants "Haaa," following the breathing speed of the receiver.

g. Next, the giver begins at the inside, and runs the palms several times outward along the meridians.

h. Remove the hands and relax.

2. Activation Exercise Using Cool Breath

a. The receiver lies down comfortably, face down, or may sit if desired. The giver sits to the side. Breathing is natural and peaceful, eyes closed or gently open.

b. The giver encourages the receiver to lie naturally and not to stretch out very much. The giver begins by holding the palms 1 inch from the body and running the palms in an inward direction to stimulate contraction—from the feet up the legs several times, from the base of the spine to the neck, from the hands up to the shoulders, and from the top of the head down to the back of the neck, and several times.

13 2b. Run palms upward.   **14** 2b. Run palms inward.   **15** 2c. Push in between fingers.

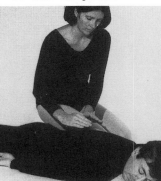

c. Using the fingers, the giver gently pushes up in the valleys between all the fingers and toes, emphasizing a gentle but firm compacting motion.

d. At the back of the neck, give a cold, yin, focused breath with the sound "Whooo." This yin stimulus to the nervous system causes a yang, contractive response, resulting in a feeling of alertness, and an activation of our heat-producing ability. For best results, the giver may blow the cold breath while the receiver is breathing *in*. Give the

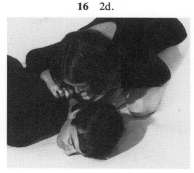

16 2d.

Apply cold breath to back of neck.

cold breath several times.

e. Press the center points of the palms and soles of the feet, to activate the nervous system.

f. Remove the hands and finalize.

3. Taking in Heaven's and Earth's Force. This exercise uses variations of yin and yang meditation, as we learned in Chapter 3, along with breathing to draw in energy from Heaven and Earth.

a. *Receiving energy from Heaven*: We sit in the Seiza or other straight, comfortable posture, breathing naturally with eyes closed or gently open, look-

17 3a.

18 3b.

Receiving Heaven's force

Receiving Earth's force

ing generally down. Hold the palms up at about shoulder level. Then, begin yang breathing, with the exhalation longer than the inhalation. Breathe in a downward direction. The abdomen moves outward on the inhalation. Chant "A-U-M" if desired. Continue two to three minutes, drawing in yang energy from the sky.

b. *Receiving energy from the Earth*: We sit in the Seiza or other straight, comfortable position, breathing naturally with eyes closed or open, looking generally upward. The hands are extended down toward the Earth. Then begin to practice yin breathing, with emphasis on the upward motion and with the inhalation longer than the exhalation. Chant "Ahhh" if desired. Continue two to three minutes, drawing in yin Earth's force.

c. *Increasing both Heaven's and Earth's force*: We

19 3c.

Breathing in a yin, upward manner to increase Earth's force

122

20 3c.

Breathing in a yang, downward manner to increase Heaven's force

sit in the Seiza or other straight, comfortable position, breathing naturally with eyes closed or half open, looking naturally forward. When breathing in, we emphasize the upward feeling as in yin meditation, and raise our hands up to follow the

The Upward Energy of Yin Breathing   *The Downward Energy of Yang Breathing*

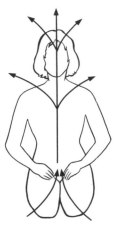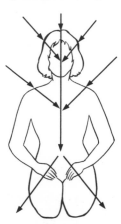

21 4b.

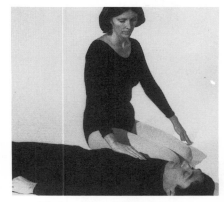

Yin breathing while giving palm healing to the right lung

movement of Earth's force. When breathing out, we emphasize the downward feeling as in yang meditation, and hold our hands down to follow the movement of Heaven's force.

(*Note*: in step *c*, the hands are used to create *movement* up or down rather than to *draw in* energy. However, you may also try the variation of holding the hands up or down as described in steps *a* and *b*.) Continue for several inhalations and exhalations, increasing the flow of both Heaven's and Earth's forces.

4. Yin Breathing During Palm Healing.

In this exercise, we use yin breathing to draw in more Earth's force during palm healing. This may be done to benefit a certain organ or part of the body that is too yang and contracted. It is often helpful for the organs that are naturally more nourished by Earth's force, such as the liver. (A discussion of Heaven's and Earth's forces in specific organs is found on the following pages, and a basic discussion is found in Chapter 6.)

   a. The receiver sits or lies down comfortably and the giver sits at the side. Breathing is natural and peaceful, eyes may be closed or gently open. The receiver's hands may be in the lap, relaxed, or in the Unifying Position. The giver begins with hands in the Unifying Position for a moment.

b. The giver places one hand on the organ or region needing care. The other hand may be in the lap, or held toward the Earth. The giver breathes with an upward, yin motion and with the inhalation longer than the exhalation. Chanting an open sound such as "Ahhh" may be added if desired. The receiver may relax quietly breathing in a somewhat yin manner also, and may chant if desired as well.

c. Continue two to three minutes, allowing the relaxed, open feeling of yin, Earth's force to develop.

d. Remove the hands, finalize, and relax.

5. Yang Breathing During Palm Healing.   Yang breathing during palm healing draws in more Heaven's force, and may be used to benefit an organ or region of the body that is too yin, expanded and loose. Organs that naturally have a greater amount of Heaven's force in their makeup are especially benefited.

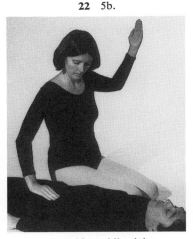

22   5b.

Yang breathing while giving palm healing to the descending colon

a. The receiver sits or lies down comfortably and the giver sits at the side. Breathing is natural and peaceful, eyes may be closed or gently open. The receiver's hands may be in the lap, relaxed, or in the Unifying Position. The giver begins with hands in the Unifying Position at first.

b. The giver places one hand on the organ or area needing care. The other hand may be in the lap, or held up at shoulder level to draw in Heaven's force. The giver breathes with a downward, yang movement and with the exhalation longer than the inhalation. Chanting a contracted sound such as "Iii" (eee) may be used, or a full sound like "Ohhh" or "A-U-M." The receiver may relax quietly, breathing naturally in a more yang manner, and may also chant if desired.

c. Continue two to three minutes, allowing the yang, Heaven's force to flow and a more warm, stable, and unified feeling to develop.

d. Remove the hands, finalize, and relax.

Note: In exercises 4 and 5, of course both Heaven's and Earth's force are flowing; we gear the exercise toward *more* of one or the other.

6. Using Yin or Yang Breathing with Complementary Organs.   We can use yin or yang breathing methods to emphasize the energy flow to one organ of a complementary pair. During palm healing exercises for complementary organs, one hand is on the more yin organ of the pair, the other hand is on the more yang organ. Depending on what type of breathing we use, we can send more energy to one organ or the other.

a. The receiver sits or lies down, breathing naturally, eyes closed or gently open, hands relaxed, or in the lap, or in the Unifying Position. The giver sits at the side, also breathing naturally and begins with hands in the Unifying Position.

b. The giver places one hand on one organ and the other hand on its complementary organ. The giver breathes in synchronization with the receiver, naturally and peacefully, and may chant if desired.

c. To draw more energy to the organ that is more nourished by yin energy, the giver begins breathing in a yin manner—upward motion, inhalation longer than the exhalation, and with a peaceful feeling. The receiver may breathe naturally, or may also make his or her breathing more yin. Chanting an open sound such as "Ahhh" may be added.

23 2b–c.

Palm healing for the right lung and left side of the large intestine; yin breathing draws energy up to the lungs.

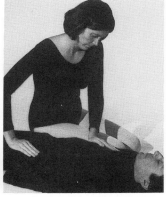

24 2b–c.

More yang breathing draws energy down to the large intestine, in the same exercise.

d. To draw energy to the organ that is more nourished by yang energy, the giver begins breathing in a yang manner—downward motion, exhalation longer than the inhalation, and with a stable, active feeling. The receiver may relax or may participate in yang breathing, as desired. Chanting may be added if desired, using a yang sound such as "Mmm" or a full sound like "A-U-M."

e. Remove the hands, finalize, and relax.

These breathing exercises represent some of the basic ways to use the breath in palm healing. Many other exercises may be created using these principles. We may also add exercises for yin and yang meridians, for example, for special situations and circumstances. By mastering the basic principles, it is possible to then go on to discover many more uses of the breath.

Yin and Yang Energy in Our Organs

As we discussed in Chapter 6, each organ has its unique proportion of yin, Earth's force, and yang, Heaven's force. Organs that are yang and compact in physical structure, are more nourished by yin Earth's energy, while organs that are yin and hollow in structure, are more nourished by yang, Heaven's energy. That is why in palm healing, we generally care for a yin or yang organ with its opposite type of energy.

Looking at the pairs of yin and yang organs in the list in Chapter 6, we see that organs nourished by Earth's force are located more on the right side of the body, which has a stronger flow of Earth's force; and organs that are nourished by Heaven's force are located more on the left side of the body, which has a stronger flow of Heaven's force. (Of course, we are speaking in general terms. All organs and both sides of the body have *both* Heaven's and Earth's forces. We are referring to the larger *proportion* of Heaven's or Earth's force in each one. An organ nourished more by Earth's force must also have a certain amount of Heaven's energy flow to be healthy.)

There are some variations to this right side versus left side principle, as shown in the following list of organs and their yin and yang energy qualities; we find some organs on the right side of the body, normally associated with more Earth's force flow, that have a larger proportion of Heaven's force, and vice versa. These variations are due to differences in the degree of yin or yang qualities, differences in organ structure and function, as well as the exact position of the organs in the body.

As a general rule, however, taking these differences into consideration, we can say that left-side organs generally show more Heaven's force, while right-side organs generally show more Earth's force.

Organ	Dominant Structure	Dominant Energy	Variations
Lungs	Yang	Earth's force (yin)	Right lung—more Earth's force Left lung—more Heaven's force
Large Intestine	Yin	Heaven's force (yang)	Right side—more Earth's force Left side—more Heaven's force
Heart	Yang	Both Earth's and Heaven's force	More Earth's or Heaven's force, depends on physical condition.
Small Intestine	Yin	Heaven's force (yang)	Right side—more Earth's force Left side—more Heaven's force Middle—depends on condition
Kidneys	Yang	Earth's force (yin)	Right side—more Earth's force Left side—more Heaven's force
Bladder	Yin	Heaven's force (yang)	
Spleen-Pancreas	Yang	Earth's force (yin)	Located on left side, but more Earth's force due to complementary function with stomach[2]
Stomach	Yin	Heaven's force (yang)	
Liver	Yang	Earth's force (yin)	
Gallbladder	Yin	Heaven's force (yang)	Located on right side, but more Heaven's force due to complementary function with liver[2]

---

[2] Note that these two pairs of organs, Spleen-Pancreas/Stomach and Liver/Gallbladder, have less polarity or difference in their yin-yang qualities than some other pairs, such as the Lung/Large Intestine which have a greater difference and show a stronger polarity or attraction.

A detailed study of the qualities of our organs' energy flow reveals that many variations exist depending on the overall physical condition and other factors. We cannot approach palm healing, therefore, in a mechanical way, by simply following a list of expected results. It is necessary to develop the innate sensitivity which we all have in order to be able to notice the energy flow ourselves and adjust our palm healing practice accordingly.

However, we may use these categories as guideposts and as a starting point for learning the practice of palm healing. In a large sense, the broad categories of yin and yang hold true, and are very helpful for guiding our study and learning.

We can use the general principles as our primary guidelines and use the variations when further refinement is needed. For example, when practicing palm healing for the lungs, we can expect that the lungs will have a greater flow of Earth's force, since they are a pair of more yang organs by structure. When doing palm healing for the left lung, however, we may notice that more Heaven's force is present. We may also notice that more Heaven's force is operating if the person is very contracted or yang. We may feel the need to add more Earth-force practices to compensate. If the person's overall condition is too yin, on the other hand, he or she may need more Heaven-force exercises, even though the basic nature of the lungs is to operate with more Earth's force. It depends on the circumstances.

As another example, let us consider the small intestine, a hollow, yin organ with a predominantly yang energy flow (Heaven's force). If we are working on the right side of the small intestine, however, we need to give more care with Earth's force to nourish that side of the organ. We will need even more Earth's-force type of exercises if, in addition, the person has a yang, contracted condition. Again, it depends on the circumstances.

We wish to avoid the idea that a computer is needed to determine these various proportions of yin and yang. It would be impossible to intellectually analyze all of these variables in advance. We suggest using the broad, general principles for guidelines, and using these variations and details to increase our understanding of how nature is operating, and to develop our sensitivity and awareness to the fluctuations of energy.

Right and Left Differences

In general, we have recommended using the stronger hand for the more important positions in palm healing. A right-handed person would use the right hand more, and a left-handed person would use the left hand more, since with our stronger hand we can generally give more energy. However, there are also differences between the right and left hands, and we can make use of these during palm healing.

The right side of our body has a stronger flow of Earth's force and the left side of our body has a stronger flow of Heaven's force. Therefore we tend to provide more Earth's force through our right hand, and more Heaven's force through our left hand. We can use one hand or the other as a variation when more yin or yang energy is needed:

- By using the right hand on organs that are nourished more by Earth's force or are in need of Earth's force;
- By using the left hand on organs that are more nourished by Heaven's force or are in need of Heaven's force;
- By using the right hand on the right side of the body, and the left hand on the left side of the body to generate more energy;
- By using the left hand on the right side of the body, and the right hand on the left side of the body to decrease excess energy.

When we intend to harmonize the whole body's energy, we continue to use our stronger hand, which tends to provide more energy than our weaker hand.

7. Palm Healing Using Right-Left Hand Differences.

a. The receiver sits or lies down comfortably; the giver sits at the side. Breathing is natural and peaceful and eyes are closed or partly open. The receiver may hold the hands in the lap, or relaxed, or in the Unifying Position. The giver begins with hands in the Unifying Position.

b. The giver selects an organ that has more Earth's force flow and places the right hand gently upon it, or held 1/2 to 1 inch above the body. Let energy flow two to three minutes. If desired, add yin-style breathing and chanting.

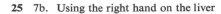

25 7b. Using the right hand on the liver   **26** 7c. Using the left hand on the stomach

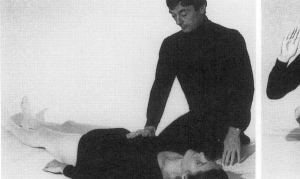
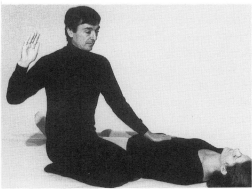

c. Next, the giver selects an organ that has more Heaven's-force flow and places the left hand there. Use yang-style breathing and chanting if desired.

d. Try several different organs, some with more Earth's force, some with more Heaven's force. Let the giver and receiver both notice the differences.

e. Now, as an experiment, try using the other hand to see whether there is a feeling of decreasing energy. Try the right hand on an organ with more Heaven's force, and try the left hand on an organ with more Earth's force.

f. Smooth the whole body's energy, finalize, and relax.

Spirals

We have seen the beneficial effects of spirallic hand motions over the head to harmonize the whole body's energy (Chapter 4). In that exercise, we used a counterclockwise spiral over a man's head to strengthen the flow of yang Heaven's force, and a clockwise spiral over a woman's head to strengthen the flow of yin Earth's force. Spirallic motions may be used in many other ways in palm healing as well. There are a number of factors that determine the yin or yang quality of a spirallic movement:[3]

Factor	Yin Effect (Earth)	Yang Effect (Heaven)
Direction of spiral:	Clockwise	Counterclockwise
Speed of movement:	Slow, gentle	Fast, vigorous
Size of spiral:	Large, expanded	Small, contracted
Up/down motion:	Hand rises up	Hand lowers down

Some Examples of Spirals: (a) Clockwise, (b) Counterclockwise, (c) Large, (d) Small, (e) Rising, (f) Descending

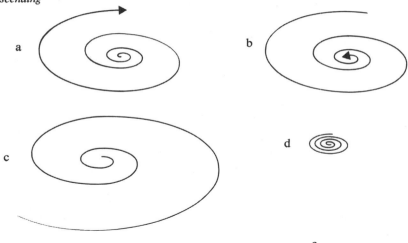

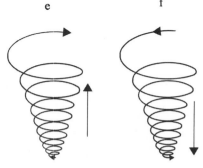

In the case of the head spiral, men and women show a different direction as described above. The bodily organs, however, are not different in men and women in terms of spirallic direction.

Spirallic motions of the hands are one of the factors we can add to our palm healing practice as a refinement, and the following exercises give some examples of how they can be used.

---

[3] The information given here is for the Northern Hemisphere. Please note that for the Southern Hemisphere, these directions are reversed.

8. Fast and Slow Spirallic Movements. Rapid motions have a more activating, energizing effect and slow movements have a more peaceful, soothing effect.

a. The receiver can lie down comfortably, or sit if preferred. The giver sits at the side. Breathing is natural, eyes are closed or partly open. The receiver relaxes with hands at the sides or in the lap. The giver begins with hands in the Unifying Position.

b. The giver holds one palm about 1/2 to 1 inch above the receiver's body, and begins at the sixth chakra or midbrain (third eye), making a slow, peaceful spiral in a clockwise direction, giving the effect of more yin, Earth's force. Continue thirty seconds to one minute; then move down to the next chakra, the throat, and repeat. Do the same at the heart, stomach/solar plexus, and abdominal chakras.

c. Next, the giver again begins at the sixth chakra, but this time, makes spirals in a counterclockwise direction with a brisk, rapid motion. This gives the effect of more yang, Heaven's force. Try this at each chakra as listed above, but only ten to fifteen seconds this time for each.

d. Smooth the whole body's energy, finalize, and relax.

9. Large and Small, Upward and Downward Spirals.

a. The receiver sits or lies down comfortably and the giver sits at the side. Breathing is peaceful and natural and eyes are closed or gently open. The receiver's hands may be relaxed at the sides or in the lap. The giver's hands are in the Unifying Position for a moment.

b. The giver holds one palm 1/2 to 1 inch above the receiver's sixth chakra (midbrain or third eye). Begin to move the hand in a clockwise spiral, and gradually let the spiral become bigger and bigger, keeping the movement peaceful and slow. Try this three to five times, and giver and receiver can both notice the effect.

c. Next, beginning at the periphery of this spiral, begin to move the hand in the opposite direction. Make a counterclockwise spiral, and gradually let the spiral become smaller and smaller. Try this three to five times.

d. Now make the expanding, clockwise spiral again as in step *b*, but this time, as the spiral expands, move the hand gradually upward, 10 to 15 inches above the body.

e. Now repeat step *c*, making the counterclockwise spiral, but begin the spiral 10 to 15 inches above the body and slowly move the hand down as the spiral contracts.

27   9d.   Expanding, rising spiral

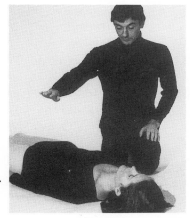

28   9e.   Conctracting, descending spiral

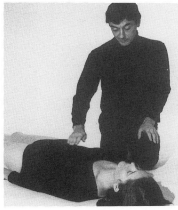

130

f. Finalize to let the receiver feel orderly and balanced. Repeat one of the spirals that accomplishes this for the receiver. Remove the hands and relax.

b—Clockwise expanding spiral
c—Counterclockwise contracting spiral
d—Rising, clockwise expanding spiral
e—Descending, counterclockwise contracting spiral

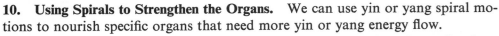

Variations:
- Experience being both giver and receiver.
- Try these spirals at a faster speed to see the effect.
- Try moving your hand opposite to the directions indicated to see the difference.
- With each variation, finish by repeating an orderly, balanced motion to avoid confusion for the receiver.
- For the expanding spirals, add yin breathing and chanting to emphasize the Earth's-force effect and for the contracting spirals, add yang breathing and chanting to emphasize the Heaven's-force effect.

10. Using Spirals to Strengthen the Organs. We can use yin or yang spiral motions to nourish specific organs that need more yin or yang energy flow.

29 10b.

30 10b.

Making an expanded, rising spiral over the liver

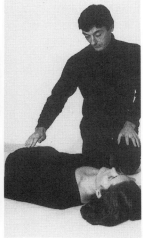

Making a contracting, descending spiral over the descending colon

a. The receiver sits or lies down comfortably, eyes closed or gently open and the giver sits at the side. Breathing is peaceful and natural.

b. The giver holds one palm 1/2 to 1 inch above the receiver's body, at the location of an organ that needs care. Determine if the organ is nourished by more Heaven's force or Earth's force. (Refer to list if needed.)

If Earth's force is needed, make a clockwise spirallic motion. It may also be a rising spiral, and you may add yin breathing and chanting as well.

If Heaven's force is needed, make a counterclockwise spirallic motion; it may be a descending spiral, and you may also add yang breathing and chanting if desired.

Make the spiral several times or one to two minutes, as desired.

c. As an experiment, try several organs, varying the spiral movements according to the yin or yang needs of the organ.

d. Also try spirallic movements at the chakras. The upper chakras tend to be more expanded and are more strengthened by larger spirals; the lower chakras, more contracted, tend to be more nourished by smaller spirals.

e. Finalize, remove the hands, and relax.

11. Using Spirals to Reduce Excess Energy. If an organ has an excess of its characteristic energy, we do not want to further nourish it with the same energy. Rather, we want to reduce or counteract that excess. We can do this by introducing the opposite type of energy. Using the opposite type of spiral is an effective way of reducing the characteristic energy for an organ.

a. The receiver sits or lies down comfortably and the giver sits at the side. Breathing is natural, eyes may be closed or partly open.

b. Identifying an organ that has an excess of energy, the giver begins by placing the palm 1/2 to 1 inch away from it. If it has too much Earth's force, use a counterclockwise spiral to introduce more Heaven's force. If it has too much Heaven's force, use a clockwise spiral to introduce more Earth's force. You may use rising or descending, large or small motions in addition, as well as yin or yang breathing and chanting to emphasize the type of energy needed.

c. Try several organs in this manner. Notice the different effects of energy flow for both giver and receiver.

d. Smooth the whole body's energy, finalize, and relax.

Additional Suggestions. The refinements and variations for palm healing practice presented in this chapter offer many opportunities for study and experimentation. They serve to illustrate basic principles and provide examples of the many things that can be done through the art of palm healing.

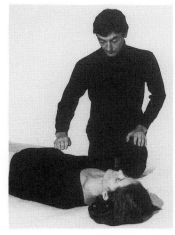

Yangizing spiral over the liver to reduce excessive yin energy

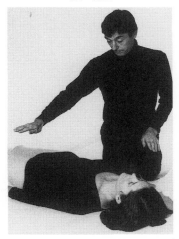

Yinnizing spiral over the descending colon to reduce excessive energy

To derive the most benefit from these techniques, we would like to repeat the suggestion given in the beginning of the chapter to use them one by one on an experimental basis at first. Allow yourself to see the effect produced by each technique without first mixing them together. Then, as you get to know their effects, begin to use these different techniques one by one and combine them in your normal palm healing practice.

These methods can make your practice more enjoyable and interesting—both to benefit your family and friends, and also as a way for study and personal growth.

Chapter 9
Comprehensive Care for Major Systems

Our body has several major systems that perform important life functions. Each system is made up of the combined functions of several organs, glands, and structures. Some of the major systems and the organs they include are listed below. Additional systems can be named as well, covering various body functions.[1]

Digestive System: Stomach, small and large intestine, liver-gallbladder, spleen-pancreas, esophagus
Respiratory System: Lungs, throat, mouth and nose, bronchi, diaphragm
Circulatory System: Heart, blood vessels, lungs; also the organs affecting blood quality—spleen-pancreas, liver, kidneys
Nervous System: Spinal column, nerve cells, brain
Immune System: Spleen-pancreas, lymph nodes, thymus gland, as well as total body strength
Reproductive System: Reproductive organs
Excretory System: Intestines, kidneys, bladder, anus

Palm healing exercises designed to benefit the whole body have an effect on each system in a general way. To provide more focused care for a particular system, we can use a series of palm healing exercises designed for that particular group of organs. We can combine a number of techniques such as the following:
- Simple care for organs
- Care for organs front/back, complementary, up/down
- Use of meridians and points
- Use of chakras related to the particular organs
- Sound, chanting, clapping
- Special uses of breathing
- Hand movements, including spirals
- Other techniques compatible with palm healing, such as Dō-In and shiatsu.

Good preparatory steps and finishing steps should be included as with all palm healing exercises.

The following exercises are examples of care for major systems. There are many possibilities for creating new exercises as well, following basic palm healing principles.

1. Care for the Nervous System. After good preparation, spend two to three minutes practicing each step:

---

[1] It is interesting to study these systems in more detail from the Oriental medicine point of view. Recommended books may be found in the bibliography.

a. Place one hand on the receiver's forehead, the other hand at the base of the spine, breathing together and chanting "Su" if desired. Allow energy to flow.

1 1. Starting posture

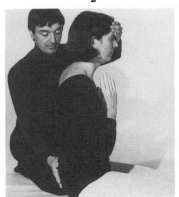

Steps *a–e*: Forehead

Step *c*: Back of head

Step *d*: Lower back of head

Step *b*: Center point between shoulder blades

Step *a* and *e*: Base of

Care for the Nervous System: Steps *a–e* One hand remains on the forehead, while the other hand touches the points as shown.

b. Keep one hand on the forehead, and move the other hand to the center point between the shoulders on the back (GV 12). Breathe, chant, allow energy to flow.

c. Next, focus on the head: place one hand on the forehead, and the other

2

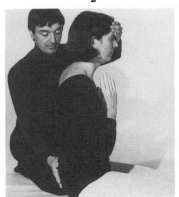

3

4

2a. Forehead and base of spine   1c. Forehead and back of head   1d. Forehead and lower back of head

on the back of the head directly behind the eyes. Breathe together, chanting if desired.

d. Keep one hand on the forehead, and move the other hand to the lower back of the head. Repeat as above.

e. Keep one hand on the forehead, and move the other hand to the base of the spine. Repeat.

f. Press strongly at the center point of the palms of the receiver's hands, several times, while exhaling (and chanting if you wish). This stimulates and energizes the nervous system, via the chakras and spiritual channel.

5

1i. Rest hand on head.

g. The center point of the soles of the feet may also be pressed as in step *f*.

h. Return to the point in step *b*, the center point between the shoulder blades (GV 12). Press this point several times, chanting if desired. This helps to calm, harmonize, and stabilize the nervous system.

i. Place one hand on top of the head, gently resting, about thirty seconds or so, breathing together peacefully and naturally, chanting if desired, to create a feeling of peaceful unification of the whole system.

j. Lift the hand off gently and relax.

2. Harmonizing the Digestive and Respiratory Systems.
Each system may be cared for alone, but complementary systems may be cared for together, reinforcing each other at the same time. Spend two to three minutes practicing each step listed below, after good preparatory steps have been done.

a. Give palm healing care to the complementary organs, lungs and large intestine, by placing one hand on the right side of the lungs, and the other hand on the left side of the large intestine. Then, change sides and repeat.

b. Using the Go points for the lung and large intestine, as shown, strongly press or give palm healing care.

c. Give palm healing care to the Yu and Sei points of the lung, then for the large intestine, and then the small intestine.

d. Run your hand along the meridian path-

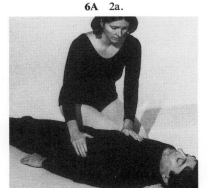

6A 2a.

Complementary care for lung and large intestine

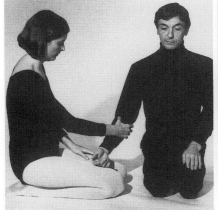
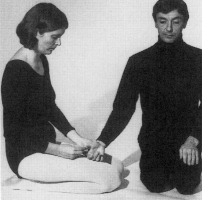

6B 2b. The Lung Go point   **6C** 2c. The Lung Sei point

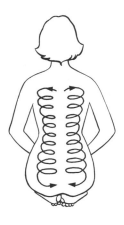

way for each organ—lung, large intestine, stomach,
small intestine. Finish by massaging the related fingertip of each one.

e. Make brisk spirallic motions over the back region,
beginning at the upper back behind the lungs, then the
middle region behind the stomach, and then the lower
region behind the intestines. Repeat these motions on
the front.

f. Finish by smoothing the energy flow gently down the
front, palms held 1/2 to 1 inch from the body. Remove
hands and relax.

3. Harmonizing the Nervous and Digestive Systems. The
nervous and digestive systems also work in a complementary/
antagonistic fashion and form the basis of our biological
functioning. This exercise gives care to each system in a way
that harmonizes them together, and builds upon the exercises

7 3a. Begin at base of spine.   **8** 3a. Moving up the spine   **9** 3a. End at the forehead.

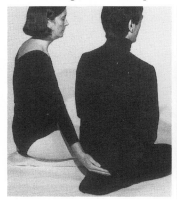
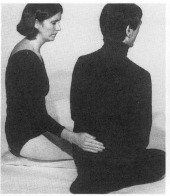
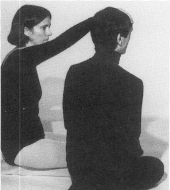

for back and front chakra care learned in Chapter 5.

a. For the nervous system, begin with your hand
at the base of the receiver's spine. Synchronize breathing, with chanting if desired.
Both persons breathe in a yin, upward manner, emphasizing the inhalation. With each
breath, move your hand about 4 inches up
the spine, then pause while you exhale. Continue until you reach the top of the head,
then go down to the forehead. We are making use of upward-moving Earth's force, so
your other hand may touch the earth.

b. For the digestive system, which is more toward the front of the body, begin with your

*Harmonizing the Nervous and
Digestive Systems*

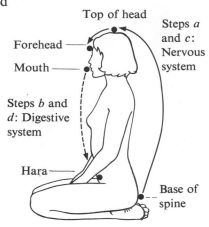

Top of head

Forehead

Mouth

Steps *a*
and *c*:
Nervous
system

Steps *b* and
d: Digestive
system

Hara

Base of
spine

10

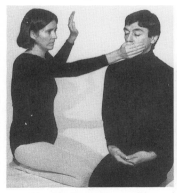

3b. Begin at the mouth.

11

3b. Move down to the hara.

12

3c. Base of spine and forehead

13 3d. Mouth and hara

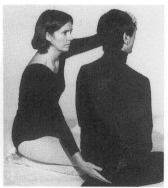

hand at the receiver's mouth, using yang breathing which emphasizes downward motion and exhalation. With each exhalation, move your hand a few inches downward, then pause while you inhale. Continue down to the hara, and hold your hand still for several breaths. Since we are making use of Heaven's force, the other hand may be raised up.

c. Now return to the back, and energize the nervous system by placing one hand on the base of the spine and the other hand on the forehead, the beginning and ending points of the nervous system. Synchronize breathing,

14 3e. Base of spine and mouth

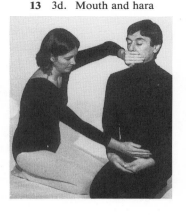

in a yin, upward manner, and chant the sound "Mmm" or "Nnn" several times, which emphasizes the heads' energy.

d. Returning to the front, energize the digestive system by placing one hand over the beginning point and the other hand over the ending point of that system—the mouth and hara. Breathe together in a yang manner, downward, chanting the sound "Su" or "Ahhh."

e. Finally, to harmonize and strengthen both systems, place one hand at the base of the spine and the other at the mouth—the beginning points of both systems. (Note that the end point of each system is not far from the beginning point of the other.) Breathe together, with normal, balanced breathing, several minutes, then slowly detach your hands and relax.

4. Caring for the Circulatory System. The receiver may sit or lie down, while the giver practices each step below for two to three minutes.

a. Grasp and press the fingertips of both hands, to stimulate general upper-body energy. Then, grasp and press the Heart Sei points at the ends of the little fingers, several times, to energize the heart.

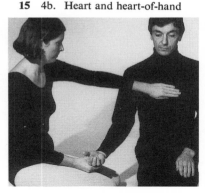

15 4b. Heart and heart-of-hand

b. Now place one palm on the heart, and with the other hand, gently grasp the receiver's hand and hold your thumb spiral at their Heart-of-Hand point in the center of the palm. Hold two to three minutes, breathing naturally and fully. Then do the same with the other hand, keeping one hand on the heart. Next, grasp both the receiver's hands gently and hold both of their Heart-of-Hand points. You may be standing behind the receiver or sitting in front to do this.

c. Now, move to the receiver's back and hold the Heart Yu points with one thumb and index finger. Then, hold the Yu points for the small intestine, the complementary organ for the heart. You may also add a variation. Sit at the side, with one hand holding the Yu points, the other holding the same Sei point. Then change sides and repeat.

d. Strengthen the energy flow of the heart by placing one palm on the heart, the other on its complementary organ—the small intestine. Breathe fully, chanting together, allowing energy to flow.

e. Make energizing, spirallic motions at the heart area, then at the small intestine area. Use a yin spiral if the person is too yang, or a yang spiral if too yin.

f. Now run your palms, 1/2 to 1 inch above the body, along the arms and legs as though to accelerate circulation, several times.

g. Sit for a moment breathing fully and naturally together, allowing energy to circulate, then relax.

5. Strengthening the Immune System.   Exercises that strengthen our whole body and blood quality are helpful for the immune system, in addition to a sound diet. We can also focus on the organs making up the specific immune functions themselves. Spend two to three minutes practicing each step below.

a. The receiver may sit in the Seiza or other straight, comfortable posture. The giver sits at the side and both breathe naturally and fully. The giver begins by smoothing the whole body's energy in preparation. Then, spend a few minutes strengthening the Triple Heater function—the three central body chakras. (See chapter 5 for a review.)

b. Strengthen the spleen-pancreas area at the middle left side of the body, with one hand on the front, the other hand on the back.

c. With one hand on the front of that same area, use the other hand to hold the spleen-pancreas Yu points on the back.

d. Then hold the spleen-pancreas Yu points with one hand, and the spleen-pancreas Sei point with the other. Change sides and repeat.

e. Then, make brisk spirallic motions down the body, beginning at the upper chest and working down to the hara, two to three times.

f. Make spirallic motions at the spleen-pancreas area.

5b. Front and back on the spleen-pancreas

5g. Thymus, front and back

g. Then, hold one palm on the thymus gland in the upper chest above the heart. Place the other hand on the back of that same area.

Location of Important Lymph Nodes

h. At the major lymph-node areas, first run your hand 1/2 to 1 inch over the body several times as though accelerating lymph circulation,

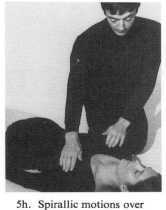

5h. Spirallic motions over underarm lymph nodes

then make brisk spirallic motions at that area, and then once again run your hand over the body several times. The lymphatic system covers the entire body, but major concentrations of lymph nodes are found in the armpits, the central intestines, and the area where the legs meet the abdomen (the groin).

i. Firmly press the Heart-of-Hand and Heart-of-Foot points, or give palm healing care there.

j. Smooth the body's energy as a whole, then relax.

The preceding exercises can serve as examples for creating series of steps to care for the organs involved in each major system, as well as for additional systems of our body.

The following exercises show additional ways of harmonizing and strengthening the energy system of our whole body, for yinnization or yangization as well as relaxation and vitalization.

6. Mobilization of Natural Abilities —Yangization.

It is helpful to stimulate our body's natural yangizing ability when we are experiencing weakness, indecision, instability, cold, or other characteristics of excessive yin. Spend two to three minutes on each step below. The receiver may be sitting in the Seiza or other straight, comfortable position. You may also do these exercises for yourself.

Yangization occurs when we emphasize downward and inward energy flow.

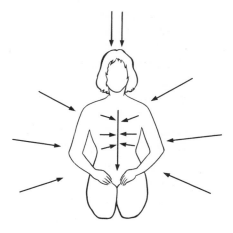

18

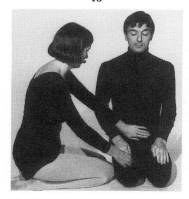

6b. Hara and Large Instestine Sei point

a. Use yang breathing, emphasizing the exhalation and downward motion; the abdomen moves in and out during this breath. We breathe as though imitating a furnace, "hah—hah—hah."

b. Give palm healing care, one hand on the hara, the other hand holding the Sei point of the large intestine, small intestine, or both (tips of the index and small fingers respectively).

c. Add chanting using the sounds "Su," "Toh," "Ah," or "A-U-M."

d. Holding the palms 1/2 to 1 inch from the body, slowly run the hands down the front and back, smoothing the energy and emphasizing the yang downward motion for stability and security and warmth. Remove the hands and relax.

7. Mobilization of Natural Abilities—Yinnization.

We can stimulate our body's natural yinnizing ability when we feel tight, tense, angry, too warm, irritable, rigid, or other expressions of excessive yang. Spend two to three minutes on each step. The receiver may sit or lie down comfortably. These exercises may also be done for one's self.

a. Use yin breathing, emphasizing the inhalation and the upward direction. This breathing imitates a cool breeze, "Whooooo."

b. Give palm healing care emphasizing upper areas of the body. For example, one hand on the lung, the other hand on the corresponding area of the head. Do yin breathing. (For a feverish condition, this can be very helpful. If the fever is due to lung congestion, place one hand on the lung, the other on the head. If due to digestive trouble, place one hand on the stomach or intestine, the other on the head.)

19 7e.

Lift palms off head.

c. Place one hand on the organ, the other on its Sei point. Hold, breathing in a yin manner.

d. Chanting may be added, using the sound "Su" or "Mmm."

e. Holding the palms 1/2 to 1 inch from the body, run the hands in a gentle, upward direction, front and back, ending by gently lifting them off the upper part of the head as though releasing pressure. Relax.

8. Relaxation Exercise. This can help to mobilize our body's natural ability to relax, and is sometimes used for insomnia.

Yinnization occurs when we emphasize upward and outward energy flow.

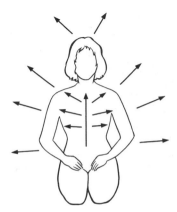

a. The receiver sits comfortably. The giver sits at the side. Both breathe naturally and peacefully, together. Eyes are closed or partly open.

b. The giver places one hand on the receiver's forehead, and the other on the base of the spine. Hold several minutes, breathing peacefully.

20 8b.

Forehead and base of spine

21 8c.

Vocal cords and hara

c. Next, the receiver may lie down (or continue to sit if preferred). The giver places one hand on the hara, the other hand on the vocal cords of the receiver. Hold two to three minutes, breathing peacefully, chanting if desired, using the sound "Su."

d. The giver then places one palm on the hara, the other on the spiral center at the top of the head, very

142

lightly touching or not touching. Breathe peacefully two to three minutes.

e. Remove the hands and relax.

9. Vitalization Exercise. This is done without a partner. It not only encourages vitality, but may increase longevity as well.

We lie down on the stomach, putting the soles of the feet together as shown. Put the palms together over the head. Breathe fully, naturally, and peacefully. In this posture, the whole body's energies are united, harmonized and reinforced.

22 8d. Hara and head spiral

Maintain this posture two to three minutes, or as desired. Remain silent, or add chanting if you wish, using a sound such as "A-U-M."

Then, return to a normal posture and relax.

23 9. Vitalization posture

Chapter 10
Comprehensive Care for Major Organs

In Chapter 6 we discussed palm healing exercises for the internal organs, using a number of basic methods. Here, we will discuss how to give especially focused care to one organ, using a series of exercises combining techniques from Chapters 5 through 8. When we give care to an organ in this intensive fashion, we strengthen its energy flow and this helps to improve its condition. Complementary/antagonistic organs are helped as well.

As in all palm healing care, in using these exercises it is important to always practice good preparation and finalizing steps, in order to keep the whole body's energy balanced.

The exercises that follow are in three categories:
A.   Exercises for Internal Organs
B.   Exercises for the Head and Face
C.   Exercises for the Mind and Emotions

A. *Exercises for Internal Organs*

1.   Comprehensive Care for the Lungs.   This series of exercises is helpful when the lungs are weak or out of balance. The receiver may sit comfortably; giver and receiver synchronize breathing, following the breathing speed of the receiver. You may also do some of these exercises for yourself. Spend two to three minutes on each step or as desired.

a.   Briskly rub and massage your own cheeks to promote stimulation of the energy flow to the lungs.

b.   Place one palm on the right cheek, the other palm on the left lung. Giver and receiver breathe naturally and fully, allowing energy to flow. Then do the other side.

c.   Now give care to the lungs and their complementary organ, the large intestine. Hold one hand on the right lung, the other on the left side of the large intestine. Hold, breathe naturally and allow energy to flow. Change sides and repeat. Chanting may be added if desired, such as "Su" or "Ahhh."

d.   Next, place one hand on one lung, and with the other hand hold the same side Lung Sei point near the tip of the thumb. Then, change sides and repeat.

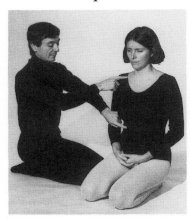

1

1e.   Lung and liver points on outer side of rib cage

Steps *e* and *f*: Lung and liver diagnosis points. X=step *e* points, dots=step *f* points.

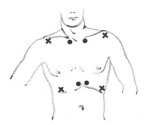

e. See the drawing showing the Lung and Liver Diagnosis points located at the upper and lower outside edges of the rib cage on both sides. First, on the right side, use the thumb spiral or finger spiral to touch the Lung point with one hand, and with the other hand, touch the Liver point of the same side. Hold, breathing and chanting if desired, two to three minutes. Then do the same with the points on the left side.

f. Next we use the central points at the top and bottom of the lung region, as illustrated. One hand holds the two central points at the top

2 1f. Central lung points

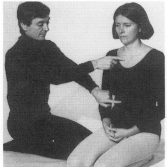

3 1g. Spirallic motions

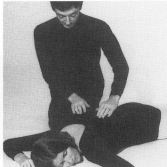

Step *g*: Brisk spirallic motions at lung area

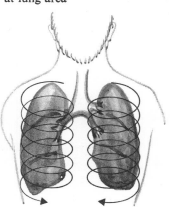

of the ribs near the throat, using thumb and index finger spirals; the other hand holds the two central points at the bottom of the rib cage.
Hold, breathe, and chant if desired. This is helpful for bronchitis as well.

g. On the back, use the palms held 1/2 to 1 inch from the body to make brisk spiralic motions at the lung area.

h. Hold one hand on the front of the right lung, the other hand on the back of the same lung. Breathe and allow energy to flow two to three minutes, chanting if desired. Then do the same for the left lung.

i. Smooth the whole body's energy and relax.

4 2a. Small intestine

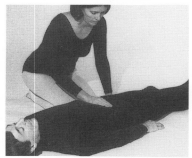

2. Comprehensive Care for the Intestines. Good intestinal function is essential for good health. In this exercise we give care to both the small and large intestine. The receiver may sit comfortably, or may lie down, turning on one side when palm healing care is given to the back.

a. Hold one palm gently on the small-intestine region, near the hara, and the other palm

5 2b. Ascending colon   **6** 2c. Transverse colon   **7** 2d. Descending colon

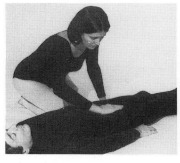 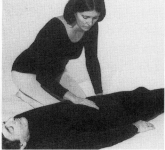 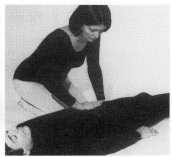

8 2e. Lower abdomen
     and rectal area

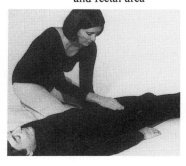

Steps *a–e*: also
shows direction
of movement for
step *f*.

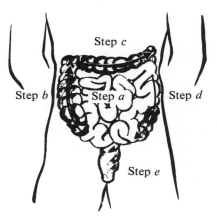

on the back at the same region. Breathe
naturally in synchronization with the receiver and allow energy to flow for about
one minute.

b. Next, hold one palm on the right side of the abdomen, the ascending colon,
and the other palm on the back at the same position, and proceed as
above.

c. Repeat this procedure for the transverse colon, just below the stomach.

d. Next, do the same for the descending colon on the left side.

e. Finally, place one hand at the base of the spine to give care to the rectum
and anus, and the other hand on the lower front of the abdomen.

f. Next, on the front, make a spirallic movement with the palm following the
same direction of movement as shown in
the drawing. This accelerates the natural
direction of the intestines.

9 2f. Spirallic movement

g. Now place one palm on the central small-
intestine area, and with the other hand,
hold the Sei point for the small intestine,
using the thumb spiral to touch the point.
Then, one palm still on the intestine, hold
the Sei point of the other side.

h. Next hold the Sei point for the large intestine while you use the other hand to touch

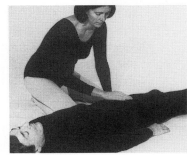

the intestinal area itself, first one minute on the ascending colon, then one minute on the transverse colon, and then one minute on the descending colon. Now hold the Sei point of the other side and repeat.

i. Now at the back, touch the Yu points for the small intestine; then the Yu points for the large intestine, each time holding one to two minutes while breathing naturally and fully, and chanting if desired, using the sound "Su," "Ahhh," or "Toh." Then, on one side, use one hand to hold the Small Intestine Yu point and the other to touch the same Sei point, then do the other side. Then, do the same for the Large Intestine Yu and Sei points.

j. Run your palms several times down the Intestine Meridian on the arms.

k. Firmly press the point Gō-Koku at the indented place near the base of the thumb on both of the receiver's hands. Do this gently but firmly several times to stimulate intestinal action.

l. Place your hands gently on the head areas corresponding to the large intestines as illustrated. Allow energy to flow one to two minutes.

m. Smooth the whole body's energy, then remove the hands and relax.

3. Comprehensive Care for the Reproductive Organs. These exercises are helpful for weakness or imbalance in the reproductive organs. They may be done for one's self or as a partner exercise. (*Note*: For vaginal discharge or menstrual irregularity, another helpful exercise is the one for the sinus in part B of this chapter, as this area is related in a complementary fashion.)

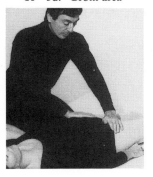

10   3d.   Groin area

a. Begin with brisk rubbing and Dō-In pounding (light pounding) on the lower back.

b. Place the palms over the kidneys on the back. The adrenal glands at the kidney area influence vitality and the condition of the reproductive organs. Breathe and chant.

c. Massage the ears, then firmly hold and release several times. The ears are related to the kidneys in a complementary fashion.

d. Place one hand on each side at the top of the thigh where the thigh joins the hip bone. Give palm healing care several minutes, breathing fully and naturally, and chanting if desired. Use the sound "Su," "Ah," or "A-U-M." This influences meridian flow for the reproductive organs.

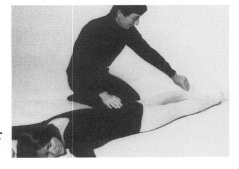

11   3f.   Lower back and Achilles tendon

e. Give palm healing care to the Triple Heater Chakras as shown in Chapter 5. Begin with the heart area and end with the hara, breathing fully and naturally. Give a few extra moments at the hara.

f. The giver places one palm on the lower back, and the other hand gently holds

12 3f. Lower back and Achilles
tendon, bent leg position

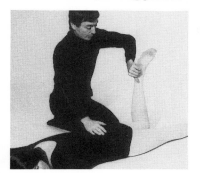

Comprehensive Care for Reproductive Organs: Steps *d* and *e*

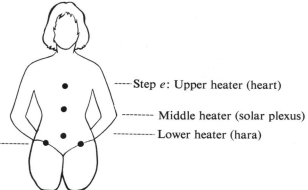

---- Step *e*: Upper heater (heart)

------- Middle heater (solar plexus)

--------- Lower heater (hara)

Step *d*: Top of ------- thigh, where thigh joins hip.

the Achilles tendon at the back of the ankle. Hold two to three minutes, breathing fully and allowing energy to flow. This accelerates the meridian flow affecting the reproductive organs. Now keep one palm on the lower back, and touch the Achilles tendon on the other side.

g. Smooth the whole body's energy flow, remove the hands, and relax.

4. Comprehensive Care for the Kidneys. Some of these exercises may be done alone, while others require a partner. The receiver may sit comfortably or lie down, turning on one side when exercises are given to the back. Both giver and receiver should breathe naturally and peacefully.

a. Briskly rub the kidneys one to two minutes, and lightly pound the kidneys as in Dō-In.

b. Place one palm on each kidney, breathing fully and chanting if desired. Allow energy to flow two to three minutes.

c. Place one palm on the back of the right kidney and the other palm on the front at the same location. Allow energy to flow two to three minutes. Do the same with the left kidney.

d. Thoroughly massage the ears, which are complementary to the kidneys.

e. With one hand, cover the back kidney area; place the other hand on the base of the spine. This helps the nervous system connection with the kidneys and stimulates nerve impulses.

f. Keep one hand covering the

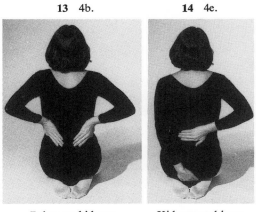

13 4b.   **14** 4e.

Palms on kidneys   Kidneys and base of spine

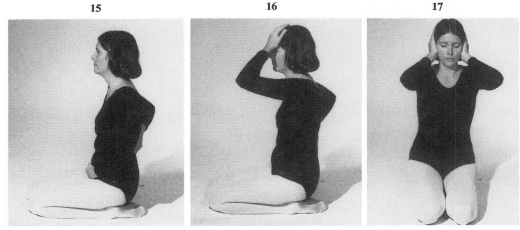

15	16	17
4f. Kidneys and bladder	4j. Kidney and side of upper forehead	4k. Cover ears.

back kidney area, and place the other hand on the bladder region in front, which is also complementary to the kidneys.

g. Place one palm on the kidney, and the other hand holding the kidney Sei point on the sole of the foot—the Heart-of-Foot point—of the same side. Then do the other side.

h. Use one hand to hold the two kidney Yu points on the back, and with the other hand, hold one Sei point on the foot. Then change and do the other foot.

i. Beginning at the base of the spine, run your palms along the kidney meridians on the legs, two to three times.

j. Now using the kidney spots at the left and right sides of the forehead, place one hand on the back of the right kidney, and the other hand on the left kidney spot on the forehead. Give palm healing care. Then, do the other sides.

k. With one hand covering each ear, breathe peacefully and chant "Su," "A-U-M," or "Ji" (the sound for the kidney) several times.

l. Smooth the whole body's energy and relax.

Using the preceding exercises as examples, you can create additional exercises for any of the organs.

B. Exercises for the Face and Head

The following exercises are very helpful for improving the condition of the nose, sinuses, ears, eyes, and other parts of the face and head. Of course, they also give an influence to the corresponding part of the lower body.

1. Exercises to Strengthen the Brain. We can use palm healing to strengthen the energy flowing through the brain, harmonizing that region, resulting in more smooth and clear brain functioning. A feeling of calm and mental stability is often experienced as a result of these exercises as well.

a. Lightly smooth the energy around the head, from the top down, several times.

b. Place one hand on the forehead and the other hand on the back of the head opposite the forehead. Hold two to three minutes, breathing naturally and

18

1a. Smoothe.

19

1b. Forehead and back of head

20

1c. Sides of head above ears

21

1d. Upper forehead on one side, lower back of head on opposite side

fully. Chant if desired, using the sound "Su" or "Mmm."

c. Place one palm on the right side of the head, just above the ear, and the other palm on the left, and hold for two to three minutes.

d. Then, place one palm on the left side of the forehead, and the other palm on the right lower back of the head, in a diagonal manner, two to three minutes. Then do the other side.

e. Once again smooth the energy around the head.

f. End with a spirallic motion on top of the head, one to two minutes, very peacefully. (For a man counterclockwise, for a woman clockwise.) Gently lift the hands at the end.

2. Care for the Eyes.   This series of exercises leaves the eyes feeling refreshed and renewed, and can help to improve vision and alleviate eye troubles. You may use all of the steps listed below, or just a few at a time.

a. Since the eyes are very sensitive, prepare the palms well, generating energy by rubbing the palms together and holding them in the Unifying Position, breathing naturally and chanting "Su" if desired.

b. Check the condition of the eyes by gently pressing two key diagnosis points

150

22 2b. Top of eyeballs **23** 2b. Inner corners of eyes **24** 2c. Self-treat with saliva

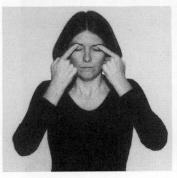  

25 2d. Palms over eyes

with the fingertips, first at the top of the eyeball in the indented place, then at the inner corner of the eye. Gently press in and if it is too painful, that indicates that the eye is swollen. (The top point measures nearsightedness, the inner corner astigmatism.)

c. Wet your finger with your own saliva and gently stroke the saliva around the eyes. Saliva is alkaline and has healing powers, especially for yin eye conditions such as cataracts.

d. Place one palm over each eye, the center of the palm directly over the eye. The eyes should be closed. Breathe slowly and peacefully, keeping this position two to three minutes. Then remove the hands suddenly as if releasing pressure. (As an experiment, do this for only one eye, and then compare how it feels with the untreated eye. Then care for the other eye.)

e. The vision center of the brain is located in the back part of the head, opposite the eyes. We may use this complementary position to strengthen the eyes' energy flow. Place one palm over the right eye, and the other palm at the center of the back of the head. Hold two to three minutes, breathing in a yin, upward manner. Then, keep one palm at the back of the head, and place the other over the left eye. Repeat. Finally, place one palm over both eyes, and the other at the back of the head. Yin breathing emphasizes the energy flowing more to the head.

Step *e*: Vision center at the back of the head   **26** 2e. One eye and back of head   **27** 2e. Both eyes and back of head

28

2f.   Top of eyeballs and back of head

f.   Next, hold one palm at the back of the head, while the tips of the thumb and index finger of the other hand gently push in at the top of both eyeballs. Give the sound vibration "Mmmm" while holding one to two minutes.

g.   Next, use the thumbs to gently but firmly squeeze the inner corners of the eyes at the sides of the nose, ten seconds, then detach quickly. Repeat five times. (This movement may also be used at the point on top of the eyeball, with the thumbs gently inserted under the upper socket, in place of step *f*.)

h.   Give palm healing care to the eyes using the principle of complementary organs, one palm over the right eye and the other palm on the liver, then one palm over the left eye, and the other palm on the spleen. In each case, hold two to three minutes, breathing peacefully.

i.   Harmonize the eyes using the meridians of the liver and spleen. First, place one hand over the right eye and the other hand on the liver Sei point, then one hand over the left eye and the other hand on the spleen Sei point. Hold, breathing naturally and chanting if desired, "Su" or "Mmmm."

j.   Finish by once again holding the palms over the eyes, two to three minutes, then remove the hands, finalize, and relax.

3.   **Care for the Ears.**   The following series of exercises is helpful for ear functions and has even been known to make deaf people able to hear.

a.   First, briskly rub the ear and the area around the ear to stimulate circulation and energy flow.

b.   Place one palm over each ear and hold two to three minutes, breathing naturally and chanting "Su" if desired.

c.   Place one palm over one ear, and the other palm over the back of the kidney on the same side, and hold for two to three minutes. Then do the other side.

d.   Gently push the long middle fingers into the ears, not too deep, and gently vibrate the fingers in and out. This helps to loosen stagnation and stimulates energy flow. Meanwhile, the rest of the fingers may lightly touch the head. While practicing this step, chant "Su" several times. At the same time, the receiver chants "Mmmm."

e.   After chanting "Su" for the last time, the giver lifts his or her

29   3d. Fingers in ears

30   3e. Look up and breathe in.

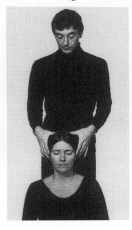

31 3e.

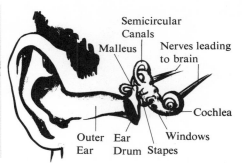

Semicircular
Canals

Malleus

Nerves leading
to brain

Cochlea

Outer Ear Windows
Ear Drum Stapes

Release fingers quickly while blowing into top of head.

Stimulus to the ear also
stimulates the midbrain.

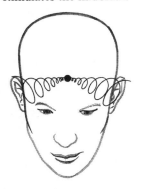

head and looks up as though drawing in energy from the sky. Then bend down and blow quickly and sharply into the top of the receiver's head, at the head spiral. Simultaneously the giver removes the fingers from the ears very fast, twisting them spirallically.

f. Finish by lightly brushing upward around the sides and back of the head to disperse any remaining stagnation.

4. Palm Healing Care for the Nose.   These exercises are helpful for the nose and air passages, as well as for the complementary organs in the lower body—the heart and lower bronchi.

a. Begin by rubbing the nose to stimulate circulation. First, rub one side of the nose with the thumb, then rub the other side with the index finger, finally rub both sides together vigorously.

b. Practice breathing through each nostril as follows to improve the circulation of air and energy. Close one nostril with the thumb, and breathe in the other nostril. Then close the other nostril with the index finger and breathe out the first nostril. Next, breathe in the same nostril. Next, close the other

32 4b.

Close nostril with thumb.

33 4b.

Open first nostril, close other nostril with index finger.

34 4c.

Tip of nose and bronchi

nostril and breathe out the first one, then breathe in the same nostril. Repeat ten times.

c. Apply one palm center to the tip of the nose, the other to the heart-bronchi region. Hold two to three minutes, breathing naturally and allowing energy to flow.

d. Apply one palm to the nose, the other to the base of the spine (the beginning of the nervous system). Hold two to three minutes, giving palm healing care.

e. Smooth the energy around the head, top down, several times. Then relax.

5. Palm Healing Care for the Sinus.

a. Place one palm over the sinus area (see illustration), and the other palm over the back of the head opposite the sinus. Hold two to three minutes, breathing fully and naturally and chanting "Su" if desired.

b. Making use of the three points illustrated, place the index finger on point #1, the thumb on point #3, and the middle finger on point #2. Breathe peacefully and naturally. The giver may chant "Su," the receiver may chant "Mmm." Hold two to three minutes, or chant about ten to fifteen times. Then, remove the hand quickly (this helps to loosen stagnation).

Step *a*: Sinus region and complementary back-of-head region

Step *b*: Three sinus points

35 5b. Sinus points

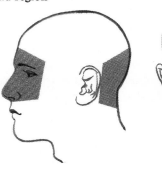

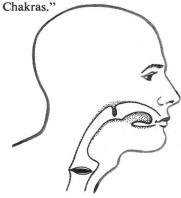

The vocal cords near the throat chakra, and the uvula in the upper throat. Energy flow is similar to illustration for Chapter 5, Exercise 8 (p. 98), "Harmonizing Head and Throat Chakras."

c. Finally, smooth the energy around the head area, remove the hands, and relax.

6. Comprehensive Care for the Vocal Cords. In our human body, the forces of Heaven and Earth meet at the region of the vocal cords, particularly the uvula at the back of the throat. If Heaven's and Earth's forces are not flowing smoothly through our body, we may have speech problems resulting from Heaven's and Earth's forces not interacting well at the vocal cords. Stuttering, voice problems, and the inability to speak (dumbness) may result. Energy problems may be caused by too much yin food or drink, making the vocal cords swollen and expanded,

154

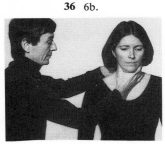

36 6b.

Vocal cords, front and back

or by a too yang condition (too much dryness or warm, heavy foods), making the vocal cords tense and tight. In either case, their free movement and the movement of energy in that region is impaired.

The following exercises are helpful to relieve these conditions and promote smooth energy flow. The receiver may sit comfortably; the giver sits or stands at the side.

a. The receiver touches the tongue to the palate (roof of the mouth), or if possible, to the uvula.

b. The giver places one palm in front of the neck, with the thumb just below one ear, and the middle finger just below the other ear. The other palm is applied to the center of the spiral at the top of the head.

c. The giver chants "Su," while the receiver chants "Mmmm." Continue two to three minutes together.

d. Remove the hands suddenly and quickly, as though briskly relieving pressure.

C. *Palm Healing Care for the Mind and Emotions*

In the wholistic sense, our mind and body are one. We have one system of energy flow that nourishes and interconnects all parts of our body, and our mind and emotions are part of this interconnected flow as well. Just as there are complementary relationships among the various organs, there are also corresponding relationships between the physical body and our mind and emotions.

Different emotions and thought patterns, like everything else in the world, show varying proportions of yin and yang energy—Heaven's and Earth's forces. Each emotion has a specific type of energy which is similar to the type of energy in a specific bodily organ. In fact, these organs and emotions are very closely linked, and the condition of the physical organ helps to produce the emotion or mental state. The following list shows the internal organs and the emotions linked with them, according to traditional Oriental medicine theory.

Organ	Associated Emotion: when balanced	Associated Emotion: when imbalanced
Heart and Small Intestine	Calm, peaceful, adaptable	Excessive talking, laughing, noisy, overactive, unpredictable
Spleen-Pancreas and Stomach	Sympathetic, understanding	Indecisive, jealous, cynical, suspicious, self-pity
Lungs and Large Intestine	Stable, practical	Depression, worry, melancholy
Kidneys, bladder and reproductive organs	Courage, interest	Fear, anxiety
Liver and Gallbladder	Patience, orderliness	Irritability, anger

Palm healing care given to a certain organ can therefore be helpful in harmonizing the emotions associated with that organ. Palm healing care given to the whole body in general, tends to bring harmony and peace to our emotional and mental state as a whole.

When we are in good condition, following a macrobiotic-quality diet and lifestyle, we tend to show the positive side of these mental and emotional states. When we are out of balance, one or more negative traits start to appear. Through correcting our diet, lifestyle, and also through the use of palm healing practices, we can restore balance.

Besides their relationship to specific organs, our emotional and mental states are also related to the major chakras of the body, as we discussed in Chapter 5. The following list summarizes the major mental and emotional traits associated with each chakra.

Chakra	Mental Attributes
First, base of spine	Physical and mental harmony with the surroundings, adaptability, stability, strength
Second, hara	Confidence, stability
Third, solar plexus	Mental power, energy, control, assertiveness
Fourth, heart	Love, both individual and universal; sensitivity, sympathy toward others
Fifth, throat	Intellectual and artistic ability and expression
Sixth, third eye	Concentrated thought, abstract thought, focus
Seventh, crown	Expansion of consciousness, universal understanding, diminishing of egocentricity

Because of these physical-mental interrelationships, we can use the art of palm healing to heal our mental and emotional state by giving care to the appropriate organs and chakras. In addition, a general whole-body type of palm healing care will help to harmonize our mind and emotions as a whole. We can use our understanding of yin and yang energies, and make use of a number of palm healing techniques to create series of exercises to balance our mind and emotions as a whole, and to give special care to specific areas.

For example, if someone needs to reduce fear and develop courage, give special exercises for the kidneys, in addition to a whole-body harmonization. If someone needs to reduce anger and develop patience, exercises are needed to calm and sooth the liver. A person experiencing indecision and suspicion will wish to harmonize and strengthen the spleen-pancreas and stomach areas.

A person wishing to develop greater confidence and stability may concentrate more exercises near the hara chakra, while someone who wishes to develop a sense of universal love for mankind may do more exercises related to the heart chakra, as well as the crown chakra.

Many kinds of exercises may be used for mental and emotional betterment using the palm healing techniques described in the earlier parts of this book. Special attention may be given to the type of breathing that is done and the mental image

156

that is maintained along with these exercises. Good preparation and finalization are equally important.

Of course, it is always helpful to practice general whole-body balancing exercises in order to develop a well-rounded energy flow with all organs and chakras operating well.

Following are additional exercises for harmonizing the mind and emotions.

1. Harmonizing the Mind and Emotions—Self-Exercise. This exercise is helpful for bringing the mind and emotions to a peaceful, clear, balanced state.

    a. Sit in the Seiza or other comfortable, straight position, eyes closed or half open, hands in the Unifying Position or folded in the lap. Breathe naturally and peacefully.

    b. Practice the preparatory exercises for clearing the aura and generating healing ability.

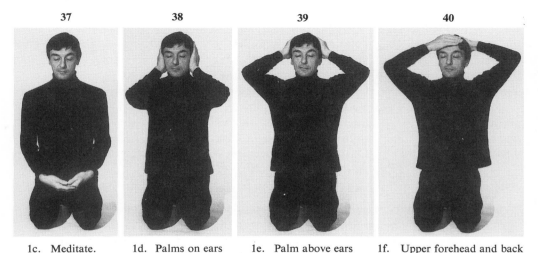

| 37 | 38 | 39 | 40 |

1c. Meditate.   1d. Palms on ears   1e. Palm above ears   1f. Upper forehead and back of head

41

1g. Top and base of head.

    c. Then, meditate peacefully for several minutes, breathing smoothly and naturally; chant if desired. The mind may be clear and empty, or focused on a peaceful mental image, or simply following the breath.

    d. Continue in this meditation while you raise your hands and place one palm over each ear, and hold for two to three minutes.

    e. Next, place the palms a little higher, just above each ear, and hold for two to three minutes.

    f. Move one palm to the upper forehead, and the other palm to the upper back of the head, and hold for two to three minutes.

    g. Now place one palm on top of the head, and the other at the base of the head, and hold for two to three minutes.

h. Then place one palm over the eyes, and the other at the back of the head directly opposite the eyes, and hold for two to three minutes.

42 1h.

43 1j.

i. Now practice palm healing Dō-In[1] on the shoulders, the heart area, the stomach solar plexus area, and the hara, as well as any other organs or areas that need attention.

j. Return your hands to the Unifying Position, clap two times, then chant the sound "Su" while breathing naturally and peace-

Eyes and back of head   Unifying position

fully, then sit quietly and relax. You may practice this exercise taking a shorter or longer period of time, as desired.

2. Harmonizing the Mind and Emotions—Partner Exercise. The following steps may be used as a series, or you may use just one or more steps at a time. The receiver and giver should both prepare well as in steps *a*, *b* and *c* of the first exercise above.

a. The receiver sits, after preparation steps, hands in the Unifying Position or in the lap. The giver sits or stands at the side. Breathe together, following the breathing of the receiver. The receiver touches the tip of the tongue to the plate (roof of the mouth) or if possible, to the uvula (hanging down in the back of the throat). The giver places one palm on top of the receiver's head, and the other hand is held up in the air. Allow energy to flow two to three minutes, while breathing naturally and chanting if desired, using the sound "Su."

b. Standing behind the receiver or sitting up on the knees, the giver takes the receiver's hands and holds the thumbs lightly, at about the receiver's shoulder

44

45

46

2a. Palm on head, other hand in the air

2b. Holding the hands

2c. Spiral over head

---

[1] Self-palm-healing: see Chapter 11.

level or ear level. Hold two to three minutes, breathing naturally or chanting.

c. Next, the giver makes a spirallic motion over the receiver's head, peacefully and calmly two to three minutes—clockwise for a woman, counterclockwise for a man.

d. Now the receiver lies down on the back. The giver picks up the receiver's feet 1 to 2 inches above the floor and gently sways them back and forth several times, then rests them again on the floor.

e. The giver places one hand on the receiver's hara, the other hand on the forehead to connect the receiver's up-down energy flow, and give a feeling of stabilization and unification. Hold two to three minutes, breathing naturally. The giver may chant if desired, and the receiver as well.

f. Finish by smoothing the whole body's energy two to three times, very gently and peacefully. Then rest several minutes before resuming daily activities.

47 2d. Swaying the feet   **48** 2e. Hara-forehead stabilization

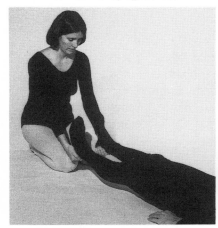
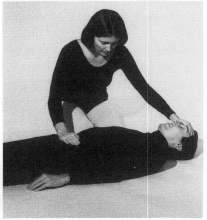

Chapter 11
Self, Group, and Distant Palm Healing

Once we have learned how to work with healing energy, it is surprising the number of ways we discover to apply it. In this chapter, we will discuss some special uses of palm healing for self-healing, for groups, and for people at a distance.

Self-Healing, or Palm Healing Dō-In

Palm healing can be done quite effectively for one's self. In several exercises earlier in this book, we have used some hand positions for self-healing. The following is a comprehensive method of self-palm healing following the pattern of Dō-In self-massage, which is a popular method related to shiatsu.[1] Using palm healing Dō-In, we can energize, calm, or generally refresh ourselves at any time, giving extra attention to areas of the body that are painful, uncomfortable, or tense.

We may use these exercises in the morning to prepare for the day, during a break in work, before dinner, or in the evening to prepare for sleep. We may use the entire series of steps in this exercise, or we may use a shorter method. Both are described below.

1. Self-Palm Healing—Comprehensive Exercise.

a. Spend a few moments calming the mind, clearing the aura and generating healing power, with natural breathing and chanting if desired. Then follow the sequence of steps listed below. You may keep your palms in each position two to three minutes, or more or less as desired, breathing fully and naturally, and chanting if desired, allowing energy to flow. Use the sound "Su" or another appropriate sound.

1

Unifying position

1. Top of the head, left and right sides
2. Left and right eyes and forehead
3. Left and right ears and side of head
4. Left and right cheeks
5. Back of neck, left and right sides
6. Shoulders, left and right (use opposite hands)
7. Lungs (upper chest), left and right
8. Lungs (lower chest), left and right
9. Kidneys, left and right on the back
10. Heart and center of small-intestine area

---

[1] See the *Book of Dō-In* by Michio Kushi.

2 Sides of head

3 Shoulders

4 Liver and spleen-pancreas

5 Knees

6 Feet

11. Large intestine, left and right sides
12. Elbows, left and right (use opposite hands)
13. Left and right sides of the waist bones in back, just below the waist
14. Base of spine and top of spine (base of neck)
15. Knees, left and right
16. Ankles, left and right

17. Toes (hold toes of opposite feet)
18. Thumbs on Heart-of-Foot points (opposite hands)
b. Finish by holding the hands in the Unifying Position, breathing naturally and fully, and chanting "Su" three to five times, then relax.

7

8

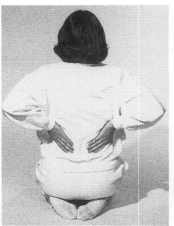

Kidneys

Base of spine and neck

2. Self-Palm Healing—Short Exercise. First, spend a minute or two if possible to calm the mind, clear the aura, and generate healing power. Then, place palms in the positions listed below. At each one, breathe fully and naturally, chanting if desired. Each position may be held one, two, three minutes, or as desired.

9	10	11	12
		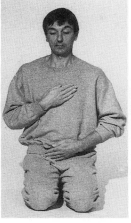	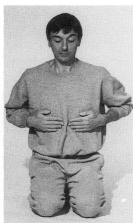
Unifying position	Lungs	Heart and small intestine	Liver and spleen-pancreas

1. Top of the head, left and right sides
2. Shoulders, left and right (use opposite hands)
3. Lungs (upper chest), left and right
4. Lungs (lower chest), left and right
5. Heart and center of small-intestine area
6. Knees
7. Feet (hold toes and Heart-of-Foot points)
   Finish with hands in the Unifying Position for a brief meditation, while breathing naturally, peacefully, and fully.

3. Self-Palm Healing—Variations. The basic self-healing exercises described above may be varied to suit your needs and the circumstances. For example:

a. Add more hand positions as needed, for specific organs or parts of the body.

13

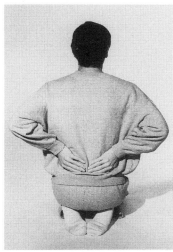

Kidneys

b. Lengthen or shorten the amount of time spent.

c. Very brief self-healing may be practiced during daily activities. For just a few seconds at a time, place your hands on your head, heart, stomach, or other area that needs care. This may be done while standing in line, waiting at a stoplight, talking on the phone, and so on. It is surprising how helpful these brief periods of self-healing can be.

Group Palm Healing

Palm healing exercises done by a group can generate a great deal of energy. They are also fun and enjoyable, and promote a feeling of unity among family and friends. Children love group exercises and it is a good way to get shy or withdrawn children to participate with a group, while angry or aggressive children seem to calm down.

When performing group exercises, it is just as important to do good preparation and finalization exercises as it is in individual palm healing work. Group members may do preparatory exercises individually—calming the mind with meditation, clearing the aura, and generating healing ability. Some of these exercises may also be done with partners or as a group. For example, the group leader may guide everyone in the beginning meditation, and aura clearing may be done by partners, as described in Chapter 4.

The exercises that follow include some methods of generating healing ability that can be practiced by two or more persons together, and a number of group exercises in palm healing for various purposes.

1.   Generating Healing Power—Creating a Magnetic Field around the Palms.
This exercise is used to prepare for palm healing. Both the giver and receiver benefit, but the emphasis is on building healing power in the receiver's hands. To fully energize both persons' palms, practice the exercise two times, changing places.

   a.   Giver and receiver sit facing each other, hands in the Unifying Position, eyes closed or partly open, breathing naturally and peacefully. If desired, chant together using the sound "Su" or "A-U-M."

14   1b.   Cup hands around palms.

   b.   The giver cups the hands around the receiver's palms, without touching, about 1 inch away, as though forming a magnetic field. Continue breathing and chanting and allow energy to flow two to three minutes. This creates a stronger energy field in the receiver's hands.

   c.   Lower the hands and relax.

2.   Generating Healing Power—Sending Energy at the Shoulders.   This exercise strengthens the energy flow through the receiver's arms and hands by joining the energy from the giver's hands at the shoulders. To energize both persons' palms, do this exercise two times, changing positions.

   a.   The receiver sits in a chair or on a low cushion. The giver stands or sits up on the knees at the back. Both begin with hands in the Unifying Position, eyes closed or partly open, breathing fully and naturally, chanting if desired.

15 2a. Preparing

16 2b. Sending energy at the shoulders

b. The giver lightly places the palms on the receiver's shoulders, allowing energy to flow two to three minutes, continuing the synchronized breathing and chanting if desired. At the same time, you may visualize the pathway of energy flow.

c. Remove the hands, take the Unifying Position for a moment, then relax.

Step *b*: The path of energy flow while generating healing ability in this exercise

3. Generating Healing Ability—Sending Energy at the Elbows.

Several points are located near the elbows which accelerate the meridian flow. By placing the palms at the elbows, the giver adds more energy flow to the receiver's palms. Practice this exercise two times, changing places to energize both persons' palms.

a. Giver and receiver sit facing each other, hands in the Unifying Position, breathing naturally and peacefully and chanting if desired.

b. The receiver keeps the hands in this posi-

Step *b*: The path of energy flow while sending energy at the elbows

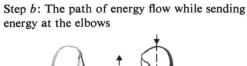

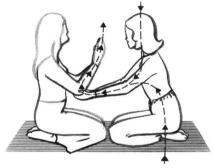

17 3b. Sending energy at the elbows

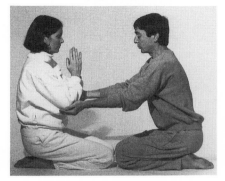

tion, with elbows raised. The giver gently holds the receiver's elbows, the center of the palm touching the end point of the elbow, not using pressure. Keep this position two to three minutes, chanting if desired. You may visualize the energy flow.

c. Lower the hands and relax.

4. Group Circle—Sending Energy Back to Front. In this exercise, energy flows from person to person around the circle through the back. Each person experiences an increase in energy, and the group is united in one continuous energy flow. If the group is very large, you may want to form two or more circles. (If desired, this exercise may be done in a straight line as a variation.)

a. Everyone forms a circle, sitting in the Seiza or other position, or in chairs. Face to one side in the same direction, allowing enough room between people so that each one can extend the arms in a relaxed fashion without touching the next person's back, but with about 1 inch of space. (Facing to the right, with the right arm on the outside, creates a counter-

18 4a. Form circle, sit quietly.

19 4b. Unifying position generate energy.

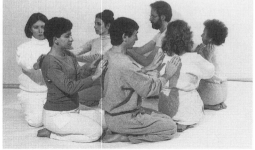

20 4c. Extend hands.

clockwise flow and introduces more yang, Heaven's force. Facing to the left, with the left arm on the outside, creates a clockwise direction of flow and introduces more yin, Earth's force.)

b. After getting into position, everyone begins with hands in the Unifying Position, breathing naturally and peacefully, eyes closed or half open, one to two minutes. The group may chant "Su" together three to five times to synchronize breathing, and unify energies.

c. Then, everyone extends the hands forward,

Step *c*: Energy flow through a Group Circle

not stiffly but in a relaxed fashion at about a 45-degree angle. Aim the palms at the center of the back (heart chakra) of the next person. Fingers are not spread wide apart, but are held loosely together. Continue to chant together (or breathe peacefully) two to three minutes, allowing energy to flow. You may also visualize the energy flow around the circle.

  d. Lower the hands, sit quietly for a moment, and relax.

Variations.   While practicing the preceding exercise, try the following variations for sending energy through the hands. See the effect of each different way.
  1. Extend the palms forward, not touching the back, with chanting.
  2. Extend the palms forward, not touching the back, but without chanting.
  3. Extend the palms forward, touching the back lightly, and chanting.
  4. Extend the palms forward, touching the back lightly, but not chanting.
  5. Now try all of the above variations using only one palm to send energy. The other hand may rest in the lap.

5.   Group Line—Sending Energy through the Fingertips.   In this exercise, energy flows through the arms and passes from person to person at the fingertips, the spiral points near the end of the fingers. (This exercise may also be done as a circle if desired; in that case, eliminate the instructions for the end people.)
  a. Everyone forms a line, sitting side by side. If the group is very large, form two or more lines. Allow enough space between individuals so that each one can comfortably link hands with the next person.
  b. When in place, everyone begins with hands in the Unifying Position for a moment to calm the mind and unify energies. Eyes are closed or partly open and breathing is natural and peaceful. If desired, chant "Su" together.
  c. Now, extend hands to the sides and link fingertips with the next person. (See illustration.) This is done so that the spiral points are lightly touching, rather than the actual tip of the finger. Have the right hand on top and the

21   5b.   Unifying position

22 5c.
Link fingertip
spirals.

Step *c*: Linking fingers at the spiral points

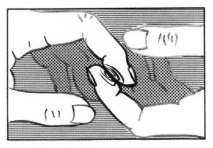

left hand underneath. At the ends of the line, the person on the right end raises the right hand up to attract Heaven's force, and the person on the left end lowers the left hand down to attract Earth's force. (The right hand has a stronger flow of Earth's force and so will attract more Heaven's force, and vice versa.) Hold this position two to three minutes, breathing naturally and chanting if desired, using the sound "Su" or "A-U-M." Allow energy to flow along the line, nourishing each person and creating harmony and unity in the group.
   d. Lower the hands and relax.

Variations. While practicing this line exercise, try the following variations:
   1. Let the end people change places from time to time so that everyone can experience each end position.
   2. Practice step *c* using chanting, but no mental imagery of the energy flow.
   3. Practice step *c* without chanting, but keeping a mental image of the energy flowing through the line.
   4. Let just one or two people chant, while everyone else remains silent, with empty minds.
   5. Let just one or two people create a mental image, while everyone else just keeps an empty mind or concentrates on the breathing.
Notice the different effects produced by each variation.

Variation 3: Mental image of energy flowing through the line

6. Group Palm Healing in a Spiral. This exercise makes use of the energy of spirallic movement. Depending on the direction the group faces, we can form a more yin spiral or a more yang spiral to accentuate more Heaven's or Earth's force. If the group faces in toward the center of the spiral, a more yang influence is given and facing outward toward the periphery creates a more yin influence. (See the accompanying illustrations.)
   a. The group forms a line in a spirallic shape, and everyone sits so that the arms can be extended to the back of the next person, not touching, but leaving about 1 inch of space. To begin, face inward to allow the spirallic movement to go in a yang direction.

23 6b. Unifying position

b. Everyone begins with hands in the Unifying Position, eyes closed or gently open, breathing naturally, two to three minutes. The group may chant together, "Su" or "A-U-M."
c. Extend the palms toward the back of the next person, at

24 6c. Extend hands.

the heart-chakra region, two to three minutes. Breathing naturally and chanting if desired, allow energy to flow. The group may also use mental visualization of the energy flow.

d. Everyone may take turns and experience the center position of the spiral, then move to the end of the line.
e. To finish, once more place hands in the Unifying Position, sit peacefully, then relax.

Variations. While practicing this exercise, try the following variations and notice the energy effects of each.

1. Everyone turns and faces outward, creating a spiral that has centrifugal force (yin, Earth's force).
2. Try sitting side-by-side and linking fingertips as in Exercise 5, first facing one way, then the other.
3. Put a man (yang) at the outermost position of the yang, inward-moving spiral to add a further yang influence.
4. Put a woman (yin) at the center position of the yin, outward-moving spiral for additional centrifugal force.
5. For maximum energy flow in either type of spiral, alternate man–woman–man–woman in line.

Group spirals: inward-facing and outward-facing

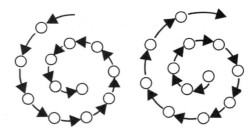

25 1. Extend hands in the opposite direction.

168

7. Group Palm Healing to Benefit One Receiver. When some member of the group is in particular need of energy, the group may practice palm healing together for that person. This creates strong, focused care and increased energy for the receiver. Care may be directed to a specific part of the body, or may be given to harmonize and energize the system as a whole.

Hands may touch the receiver, or may be held slightly apart from the receiver, about 1/2 to 1 inch. Try to avoid placing right and left hands on top of each other, as they tend to neutralize each other's energy.

If desired, group members may take turns being the receiver so that at the end, everyone in the group has been energized.

    a. The receiver may sit or lie down comfortably. Hands may be in the Unifying Position, or in the lap, or relaxed. The two or more givers sit at the side, hands in the Unifying Position. Everyone breathes naturally and peacefully, eyes closed or partly open. Add chanting if desired. The receiver may chant or remain silent. Take a moment for preparation in this way.

26 7a. Preparing

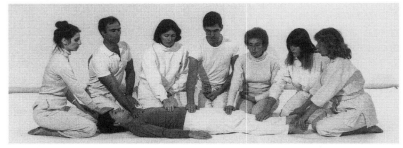

27 7c.
Palm healing for the
receiver

    b. The givers use one or both palms as needed. Begin by smoothing down the whole body's energy, two to three times together.

    c. The givers extend palms and lightly touch (or not touch) the receiver, in a coordinated manner, covering key areas that need care in a balanced, harmonious way. Organs, chakras, meridians, points, hands, knees, and feet are some of the areas that can receive care. The givers should coordinate so that their hands are placed in a harmonious manner. Continue two to three minutes, breathing together, chanting if desired. Visualization can also be helpful.

    d. Smooth the whole body's energy again.

e.   Remove the hands, sit for a moment in the Unifying Position to unify energies, then relax.

Experiment.   Notice the effect of overlapping palms as follows:

1.   Two givers overlap their right hands on the same spot. Notice the effect, increasing right hand energy.
2.   Two givers overlap their left hands on the same spot. Notice the effect, increasing left hand energy.
3.   Now overlap one right hand with one left hand and notice the neutralizing effect. (You may find this effect desirable at some times, not desirable at others.)

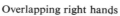

28   1.

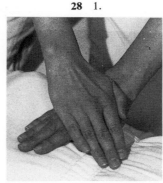

Overlapping right hands

29   3.

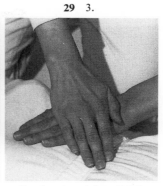

Overlapping right and left hands

8.   Group Palm Healing for One Receiver—Sending Energy.   In this exercise the givers do not touch the receiver, but send energy by palm healing at a distance of several inches. Since energy moves easily through the air, this type of healing is quite effective. Practice this exercise taking turns so that everyone in the group has a chance to be the receiver of the whole group's care.

a.   The receiver sits in the middle, and the other group members position themselves around the receiver in a circle, facing inward, allowing enough space so that arms can be extended toward the receiver with 12 inches or more space. (Try sitting one foot, two feet, or three feet from the receiver.)

b.   Givers and receiver all breathe naturally and peacefully, chanting if desired (receiver may chant or remain silent). Begin with hands in the Unifying Position, eyes closed or partly open. The receiver may place hands in the Unifying Position or in the lap.

c.   The givers extend their palms toward the receiver, first holding them at

30   8b.   Preparing

31   8c.   Extend hands toward heart.

32 8d. Move hands up toward head.　　**33** 8d. Move hands down toward base of spine.

34 8e. Return hands to heat level.

heart level, breathing naturally and peacefully, chanting if desired. Allow energy to flow for one half to one minute. If desired, you may mentally visualize the energy flowing through the palms to the receiver, and flowing in and through the receiver's energy system. The receiver can just relax and keep breathing naturally.

d.　Next, the givers slowly move the palms upward, pointing toward the receiver's head, using one full breath or chant to do this. Then, on another full breath or chant, move the palms down slowly toward the base of the receiver's spine or lower abdomen. Continue moving the palms slowly and peacefully up-and-down several times for two to three minutes.

e.　Finally, return the palms to heart level and hold them there for a moment while chanting or breathing peacefully. Then remove the hands and relax.

Variations
1.　Try sending energy toward specific locations that need care, such as certain organs or chakras.
2.　As an experiment, let the givers turn around and face outward while sending energy. Notice how everyone feels. Finish by turning back and sending toward the receiver again.

Distant Healing

As we have seen in the previous exercise, we do not need to touch the receiver in order to send energy. In fact, energy may be sent over some distance. This is possible because of the fluid, dynamic nature of electromagnetic force. Sending healing energy does not depend on how near we are to the receiver, but on how well we are managing the energy. Energy may even travel over great distances for the purpose of healing friends and family across town, in another city, or even on the other side of the world. In this case, the giver or sender acts as an energy transformer, converting the natural up-and-down energy flow to a horizontal direction, as illustrated.

To practice distant healing, we use good preparatory steps as in all palm healing practice —clearing our aura, calming the mind with meditation, and generating healing ability. In addition to the direction given to energy through the palms, mental visualization is very helpful in this exercise. Try distant healing for your relatives who live far away, and see if they experience any good results.

A. Palm healing uses hands to transform up-down energy flow to horizontal energy flow for distant healing.

B. Distant healing dynamics: Healer sends energy and positive mental image to other person, even many miles away.

1. Distant Healing Exercise. For this exercise, face in the direction of the person or persons to whom you wish to send healing force. If you do not know the location, face to the south (if you are in the Northern Hemisphere), to benefit from the flow of energy down from the north pole. (If in the Southern Hemisphere, face north.)

a. Sit in Seiza or other straight, comfortable position, breathing naturally and peacefully, eyes closed or partly open. Begin with hands in the Unifying Position.

b. As described in Chapter 4, practice calming the mind with meditation, clapping and bowing to clear the aura, and generating healing ability. Breathe fully, naturally, and peacefully

35 1a. Starting posture

36 1b. Clap.

172

37

1b. Prepare to bow.

and chant "Su" or "A-U-M," two to three minutes.

c. Now extend your palms in the direction of the person to whom you wish to send energy. Arms are not held stiffly but somewhat relaxed at a 45-degree angle as shown. Chant "Su" or "A-U-M," or just continue natural breathing. Allow energy to flow through your palms toward the receiver. You may notice some warmth or a tingling sensation in your palms. You may create a positive mental image of the person in a state

39

1b. Generate healing ability

40

1c. Extend palms.

38

1b. Bow.

of health and happiness (not in a sick or troubled condition, but as you hope they will become). Continue two to three minutes or as long as you like.

d. Lower your hands into your lap and sit quietly a moment, then relax.

2. Group Distant Healing. The same distant healing exercise may be practiced by a group for added energy. Several variations on this practice may be used as described below.

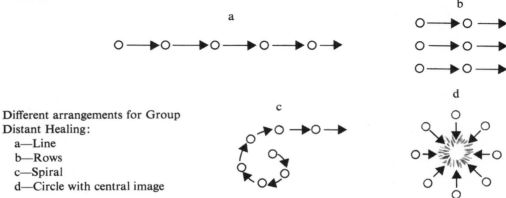

Different arrangements for Group
Distant Healing:
   a—Line
   b—Rows
   c—Spiral
   d—Circle with central image

a. The group forms a line, each person extending the palms toward the back of the next person as illustrated. The person at the front of the line extends the palms in the direction of the person to whom healing is being sent.

41 2a, b. Group lines and rows: unifying posture   **42** 2a, b. Group lines and rows: Extend plams.

43 3c. Group spiral

b. The group sits in one or more rows. Everyone faces forward and sends energy in the direction of the receiver.
c. The group forms a spiral and the end person projects energy in the direction of the person who is to

44 2d. Group circle: Unifying posture   **45** 2d. Group circle: Extend palms to center.

46 2d. Large group circle

receive the energy. Try a yang spiral and a yin spiral, as shown.
d. The group sits in a circle and everyone sends energy toward the center of the circle, at the same time with the mental image of the receiver, in a state of health, as though he or she were actually in the center of the circle.

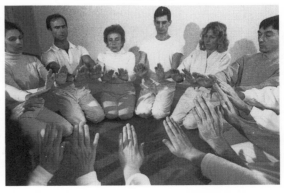

3. Sending a Protective Shield. This exercise in distant healing uses a yang, counterclockwise circle and a focused hand position to create a protective energy for someone at a distance. The receiver gains a warm, secure influence. Their energy system is firmed up, allowing them to overcome weakness and resist problems.

    a. Sit facing in the direction of the person to whom you wish to send a protective, healing influence. Begin with hands in the Unifying Position, calm the mind with meditation, clear the aura, and generate healing power. Breathing is natural and full.

Sending a Protective Shield: Circular pattern of hand movement.
    Solid line=direction as seen by an onlooker;
    Dotted line=direction as seen by you as you perform the movement (i.e., as you perform this movement, you may follow the direction of the dotted line).

47   48   49

3a. Starting posture   3b. Extend hands in focusing position.   3c. Move hands in large circle.

    b. Next, hold your hands in the Focusing Position as described in Chapter 3, hands resting in the lap, the right thumb and index finger touching the tips of the left thumb and index finger, and the remaining fingers folded. Extend the hands forward in this position, in the direction of the receiver.

    c. Now begin to send distant healing, keeping a positive mental image of the person, chanting "Su" or "A-U-M." Meanwhile, move the hands slowly in a large, counterclockwise circle as though drawing a protective line around the person. Chant at least three times, making a circle with each chant.

    d. Lower the hands and relax, keeping the positive mental image for a moment longer.

*Distant Healing
for Accomplish-
ment*: Spiral
pattern

4. Distant Healing for Accomplishment.
This exercise uses the principle of the
contractive spiral to help a person at a
distance focus and unify his or her energies. The receiver's ability to overcome
difficulties and accomplish goals is en-
hanced.

   a. Sit facing in the direction of the
       person who needs this assistance.
       Begin with hands in the Unify-

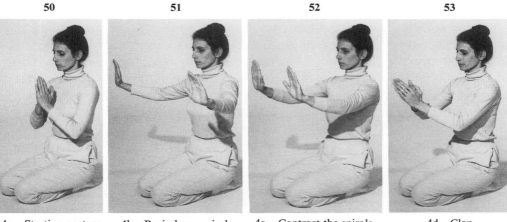

| 50 | 51 | 52 | 53 |

4a. Starting posture   4b. Begin large spiral.   4c. Contract the spirals.   4d. Clap.

ing Position, calm the mind with meditation, clear the aura, and generate
healing ability, breathing naturally and fully.
   b. Extend the palms toward the person to whom you wish to send this focusing,
       healing energy. Move the hands out a little, in order to begin making a large
       spiral with each hand in an inward direction.
   c. The first orbit of the spiral is large. Each orbit becomes slightly smaller after
       that, as the spiral contracts. When you reach the center of the spiral, each
       hand will be a little to the side, as shown. When making the entire spiral,
       chant "Su" or "A-U-M" in one long breath.
   d. When you reach the center of the spiral, give one sharp, clear clap. This
       gives a spark of energy that assists in the impetus to achievement.
   e. Repeat the spiral three to five times, each time chanting one long chant
       while making the spiral, and each time finishing with a sharp clap at the
       center.
   f. Lower your hands to the lap, sit quietly for a moment, and relax.
   The exercises given in this chapter provide basic examples for the use of palm
healing for groups, for one's self, and for friends or family at a distance. They
offer endless possibilities for practice and study, as well as for the creation of new
exercises using these as guidelines, to increase the health and happiness of our
loved ones.

Chapter 12

Toward Further Study

Palm healing can enrich our daily life both as a healing practice, and as a means of study and self-development. While we always continue to use the most simple principles of palm healing, there are a number of things we can do to improve our practice and deepen our understanding.

1. Observation of Nature and Humanity. We can increase our understanding of energy, how it works and flows by close observation of nature and humanity. Spend time observing the growth of plants, the movements of the rain and wind, clouds and weather, the sun and the stars. See how many movements are circular and spirallic, some are more up-down and some are more left-right. Notice how the different things in nature interact and influence each other, and be aware that movements of energy are underlying every phenomenon.

Similarly, notice the flow of energy in people. Energy patterns of various kinds underlie the way we move, speak, express ourselves, eat, make decisions, and so on. These energy patterns are much the same as those we see in nature. As we increase our ability to observe energy, we improve our potential as practitioners of palm healing.

2. Notice "Automatic" Palm Healing. It is interesting to notice the automatic, instinctive palm healing that we do almost constantly, without thinking about it. Try to understand why we do these things:
* Leaning on the right elbow shows the right side of the lung is weaker, as well as the right side of the brain.
* While sitting, if one leg is on top, that side is more weak.
* Clasping hands indicates striving for balance, security, harmonizing yin and yang.
* Crossing arms indicates defense and added security.
* Scratching the nose to remove excess yin from the nose indicates weakness, excess yin in the heart.
* Knocking or scratching the forehead to eliminate yin indicates the brain is too expanded.
* Rotating the head around the neck is to try to loosen stagnated energy flow.
* Knocking or rubbing the back or side of the body is to dissolve stagnant energy flow. (Notice the exact point.)
* Tapping the toes or fingers is to discharge excessive yin energy flow, toward the periphery.
* Wiggling central areas of the body such as the knees is to discharge of excessive yang energy toward the center.

- Rubbing the cheeks is to get rid of excessive yin energy from the lungs.
- One shoulder higher than the other; that side lung is expanded.
- Hands placed on the thighs is to attempt to stabilize downward-flowing energy, for added confidence.

In this way, each common mannerism and habit shows an underlying type of energy flow, and many of these involve automatic use of our hands to make balance. By becoming aware of these, we increase our understanding of how energy works.

3. Related Studies and Self-Development The best results in palm healing are gained when we are in good condition on all levels—physical, mental, and spiritual. We need to give care and attention to our daily diet and lifestyle on a regular basis, and to continue our reading, study, and practice, in a number of ways:

- Begin and maintain a good-quality diet, as discussed earlier in this book, along with exercise and healthful habits.
- Become familiar with the workings of yin and yang as an aid to understanding all aspects of our life and healing practices.
- Study anatomy and physiology. Learn the location and function of the major organs, glands, muscles, nerves, and systems of the body.
- Learn Oriental medicine theory—the meridians, points, ki flow, and Five Transformation Theory.
- Development on the mental and spiritual plane is important through meditation, religion, study, self-reflection. Emotional development is also important. Counseling, journal-writing, and other studies can be very helpful.

4. Adapting Palm Healing to Individual Needs. Like the changing, flowing nature of energy itself, palm healing is not a rigid art limited by ironclad regulations. It flows and changes with the needs of the giver and receiver, with the daily weather and circumstances, as our needs change according to what we have eaten, spoken, and done.

The principles and exercises presented in this book are intended to provide a basic introduction and understanding of palm healing so that it can be used on a daily basis. With practice and by following a lifestyle that is in tune with nature, we become more attuned to our energy and the energy of other people. Our practice of palm healing becomes very intuitive, flexible, and tailored to individual circumstances.

The exercises presented in the first few chapters of this book may appear very simple and basic, yet they contain the potentiality for many years of practice. Many people will find these beginning exercises so absorbing that they have no need to utilize any of the more complex variations. On the other hand, others will wish to use every optional method that we have presented, and will still be searching for more. Still other people will use the basic order and principles of palm healing to create their own variations and new exercises.

Whatever amount or extent you wish to incorporate palm healing into your life is totally up to you. Whether for self-healing, self-development, energy awareness, or for the benefit of your family and friends—it is here for you to use, and we hope that you will use it in health and happiness for many years to come. Palm healing is one of the ways by which we can link into our *real* healers—the energies coming to us from the sun, moon, stars, earth, the forces of nature or God, which nourish and support us everyday of our lives.

Recommended Reading and Classes

Readers may contact the Kushi Foundation for a recommendation of additional books on macrobiotics and healing, as well as certified teachers and teachings throughout the world. Their address is:

The Kushi Foundation
PO Box 1100
Brookline, MA 02147
617–738–0045

Grad, Bernard. "Healing by the Laying on of Hands: A Review of Experiments." *Ways of Health*. New York and London: Harcourt Brace Jovanovich, 1979

Krieger, Doloress, R.N. Ph. D. "High-Order Emergence of the Self During Therapeutic Touch." *The American Theosophist* (May 1984).

———. *The Therapeutic Touch: How to Use Your Hands to Help or to Heal*. New Jersey: Prentice-Hall, Inc., 1979.

Kunz, Dora and Erik Peper. "Fields and Their Clinical Implications." *The American Theosophist* (1982).

Kushi, Aveline and Michio. *Macrobiotic Pregnancy and Care of the Newborn*. Edited by Edward and Wendy Esko. Tokyo and New York: Japan Publications, Inc., 1984.

Kushi, Michio. *The Book of Do-In: Exercises for Physical and Spiritual Development*. Tokyo and New York: Japan Publications, Inc., 1979.

———. *The Book of Macrobiotics: The Universal Way of Health, Happiness and Peace*. Tokyo and New York: Japan Publications, Inc., 1986 (Rev. ed.).

———. *How to See Your Health: The Book of Oriental Diagnosis*. Tokyo and New York: Japan Publications, Inc., 1980.

Kushi, Michio and Aveline, with Alex Jack. *Macrobiotic Diet*. Tokyo and New York: Japan Publications, Inc., 1985.

Mann, Felix. *Acupuncture*. Vintage Books, 1973.

Ray, Barbara, Ph.D. *The Reiki Factor*. New York: Exposition Press, 1983.

Tompkins, Peter and Christopher Bird. *The Secret Life of Plants*. New York: Harper & Row, 1973.

The Yellow Emperor's Classic of Internal Medicine. Translated by Ilza Veith. Berkley: University of California Press, 1944.

Index